a little kitchen with a lotta flavor!

RED CARPET MENUS

Delicious Dishes Inspired
by 20 Years of Oscar®
Best Picture Nominations

Over 100 Recipes & Ideas
for Award Winning Dishes

Annette Zito

ZAMMworks
NEW YORK

works
ZAMMworks.com

ZAMMworks titles may be purchased for business or promotional use or for special sales. For information, please write to The Team, ZAMMworks, 63 Wallace Street, Tuckahoe, NY 10707.

ZAMMworks and it's logo, a bright bursting bubble with the letters ZAMM! & underscore with "works" beneath, are trademarks of ZAMMworks.

Library of Congress Publishing Data
Zito, Annette
        KitchAnnette Red Carpet Menus: Delicious Dishes Inspired by 20 Years of Oscar® Best Picture Nominations / by Annette Zito.

Includes Index.
ISBN 10: 0-9915-0110-1
ISBN-13: 978-0991501106
LCCN: 2014931963

First edition

Designed by Annette Zito

APPRECIATION & DEDICATON ELATION

This book is dedicated to my parents Antoinette and Carmelo Zito, my grandparents Anthony and Rose Giachello, and Nancy and Vincent Zito, my sisters Nancy Zito and Vincenza Zito, and my godparents Carlo and Vivian Catuogno. The richness of my life has been time spent at their tables and in their kitchens. And to my heart, Marc Mogol, who believes in me. My success is theirs.

Additionally my deep appreciation goes out to a small group who gave me guidance and assistance to complete this book through many challenges, most notably June Brewer, Anne Flynn, Randi Ginsberg, and Suzanne Sumien.

Also to my "core" people (you know who you are) and the warehouse boys who have encouraged, tolerated, and enjoyed my Oscar® madness over these 20 years. I could never have done it without them.

And finally to Joe Gulla, who was my original party co-host and without whom I'd never have started this whole thing!

CONTENTS

INTRODUCTION

The year was 1995. David Letterman was scheduled to host the Academy Awards®. Being long-time fans of Dave and his late-night talk show, my good friend, playwright Joe Gulla and I thought we should celebrate by having a viewing party.

Although I don't remember how we came up with it, Joe put together a contest dubbed the "Cool Cool Oscar Pool" and I created a menu using the Best Picture nominations as inspiration. Being a life-long "chatterbox", the one "rule" was quite ironic – no talking except during commercial breaks! Ha! We all had a great time and thought Dave did a fabulous job.

When the Academy Awards® rolled around in 1996, Joe headed to Los Angeles to see if he could wangle into any Oscar® after-parties. In honor of his efforts, I hosted again. (And yes, Joe did make it to a party!)

The format for Best Oscar® Party was born:

1. Best Menu: Create a unique menu that honors the Academy Awards® Best Picture Nominations in a full-course extravaganza – Appetizer, Main Course, Side Dish, and Dessert, with one "floating" selection (which later became a Salad).
2. Best Visual Display: Set the stage by designing parodies of the movie posters for the Best Picture nominated films to showcase the menu.
3. Be The Academy: Prior to the big show, have attendees fill out ballots for each category. The person who gets the most right is the "BIG WINNER", while the one who gets the most wrong is the "BIG LOSER" – award each a prize.

Since then, creating an Oscar®-inspired feast has become my signature event. Each year has presented new challenges. Most notably, in 2010 the Best Picture category parameters changed from 5 to 10 nominees. It was suggested that I choose only 5 from the list but I scoffed – each film would have it's own commemorative dish. The following year, it was again revised to state there would be no less than 5 and no more than 10 films nominated, which has varied the dish count each year since. I've "upped the ante" to require it be a cohesive meal that could deliciously "stand alone" without the films connection. Specialty cocktails have always been welcomed and may become a permanent addition to the festivities. You'll have to stay tuned.

To honor the milestone of 20 years, I've assembled the menus, recipes, Oscar® night food photos, & menu plaques honoring the films. Glad I kept them all! Granted, some of the selections are "a stretch" and for some dishes, I ordered out or took a shortcut, but that's part of the fun! Everything is easy to cook or I'd never make it. Substitute & adjust to your heart's content – sour cream for Greek yogurt, cheese changes, etc.

It's all good... really, really good! Join me as I take a scrumptious walk down memory lane.

Thank you for your consideration (wink!).

Annette

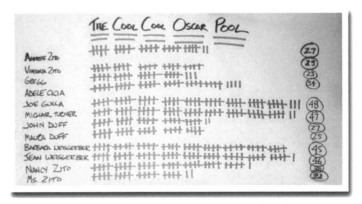

The original "Cool Cool Oscar Pool" scoreboard

1995

The 67th Academy Awards®   Host: David Letterman
The Shrine Auditorium   March 27, 1995

This is the year that got it all started! There was no plan for this to become a yearly event so it wasn't much in regard to actual recipes. Minimal cooking, maximum enjoyment!

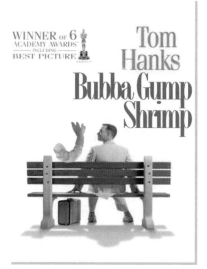

Forrest Gump – BUBBA GUMP SHRIMP

It seemed the best choice, besides the obvious "box of chocolates".

INGREDIENTS:
*   1 lb. large shrimp, cleaned
*   3-4 ribs celery, chopped
*   1 small red onion, chopped
*   2 tbsp. mayonnaise
*   salt & pepper

DIRECTIONS:
1. Boil shrimp until pink – do not over boil or they will be tough. Cool and cut into small pieces.
1. Combine shrimp, celery, onion, mayonnaise, and salt & pepper to taste. Start with less mayonnaise and add more as needed. Serve!

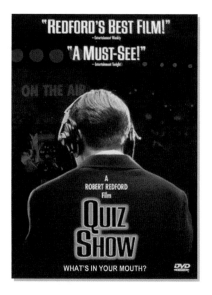

Quiz Show – QUIZ SHOW: WHAT'S IN YOUR MOUTH?

I completely blocked out what I had done for this until I found a picture with the name of this dish. I'm entirely appreciating that I was "stumped" by Quiz Show – no one had the answer! Ha! It was a variety of appetizers that were only identifiable when you took a bite. And (shame)... they were frozen.

INGREDIENTS:
*   1 package 100-ct. mixed appetizers, frozen

DIRECTIONS:
1. Prepare according to package instructions and serve.

Pulp Fiction – PENNE A LA PULP

A little tomato pulpy filetto di pomodoro with penne macaroni was just the right dish to compliment the movie.

INGREDIENTS:
- 1 cup extra virgin olive oil
- 6-8 cloves garlic, minced
- 28 oz. can whole peeled plum tomatoes
- 2 oz. basil (cut up fresh or use dried flakes)
- salt & pepper
- red pepper flakes (optional)
- 1 lb. penne pasta
- 1 cup grated Romano cheese

DIRECTIONS:
1. Drizzle oil into a large sauté pan and add the garlic on low heat until browned.
2. Raise to medium heat and add the tomatoes, crushing them one-by-one, and salt & pepper (and red pepper flakes) to taste. Stir and cover.
3. While the sauce cooks, bring a large stockpot of water to boil, add salt to the boiling water, and cook pasta according to package instructions.
4. Add a teaspoon or two of basil to your sauce as pasta cooks. When the pasta is ready, your sauce is ready too!
5. Drain pasta, add the sauce, and combine. Serve with grated Romano cheese!

The Shawshank Redemption – SHAWSHANK DU JOUR

This was a play on "bread and water" cartoon jail fare. How the world has changed - now it's considered a "crime" to love carbs. Shhhh… we won't tell.

INGREDIENTS:
- 1 loaf of crusty Italian bread
- 4 oz. extra virgin olive oil
- salt & pepper
- sparkling bottled water, chilled

DIRECTIONS:
1. Cut bread into several thick slices and place in serving basket/plate.
2. In a bowl large enough to dip the bread, pour in oil and stir in salt & pepper to taste.
3. Pour sparkling water and serve with bread and oil for dipping.

Four Weddings and a Funeral – ONE FLAVOR FOR A FUNNEL CAKE

A delicious indulgence of fried dough!

INGREDIENTS:

- 1 cup flour
- 2 tsp. baking powder
- 1/2 tsp. salt
- 2 tbsp. sugar
- 1/2 tsp. cinnamon
- 1 large egg
- 1 cup milk
- 3 tbsp. butter, melted
- vegetable oil for frying
- wax paper
- confectioners sugar

DIRECTIONS:

1. In a large bowl, sift flour, baking powder, salt, sugar, and cinnamon.
2. Stir in egg & milk. Add in melted butter and mix until well blended.
3. Using a deep skillet, add oil on medium-high heat until hot.
4. Create a funnel using wax paper and pour batter into it, holding your finger over the end until you're ready to release and drizzle into the hot oil.
5. Cook until the batter floats – bottom should be brown – and turn. When that side is also brown, remove from heat to a paper towel-covered dish to absorb excess oil.
6. Transfer to serving plate and sprinkle liberally with confectioner's sugar.

My personal party night food photo of "Penne A La Pulp":

1996

The 68th Academy Awards®   Host: Whoopi Goldberg
The Dorothy Chandler Pavilion   March 25, 1996

It was the second year of creating a menu. I still
didn't imagine this was going to be "the new thing",
but putting together the "meal puzzle" was becoming
kinda fun.

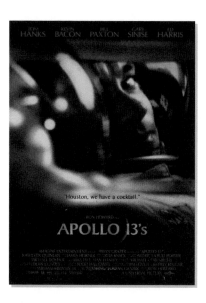

Apollo 13 – APOLLO 13'S COCKTAILS

This was the very first signature cocktail used as a "course". I don't even know if Tang is sold anymore but when I was a kid, we were told astronauts took it into space. And if you add enough vodka, you'll think you actually went to the moon!

INGREDIENTS:
- 1 package orange or grape flavored powdered drink mix
- vodka
- water
- ice cubes

DIRECTIONS:
1. Follow package instructions for powdered drink mix of choice.
2. Cut the water in half and replace with vodka.
3. Mix thoroughly and serve over ice.

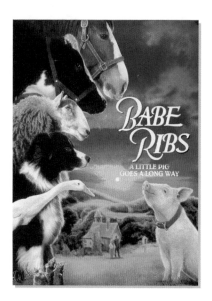

Babe – BABE RIBS

Yes, it's a bit mean but I couldn't resist having pork spare ribs! Another moment of "true confessions" – I called the local Chinese restaurant and ordered a few orders of sweet spare ribs.

INGREDIENTS:
- telephone number of great local Chinese restaurant that delivers
- telephone

DIRECTIONS:
1. Call the restaurant to order the ribs, allowing enough time for them to arrive piping hot.
2. Pay the delivery person when they arrive, tip well, plate and serve!

Il Postino – IL PASTINA

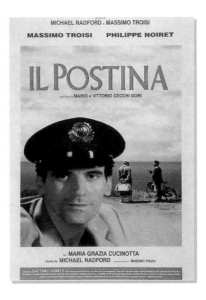

What a wonderful film that takes place on a small Italian fishing village island. The choice for this dish was obvious – shrimp in a fresh tomato sauce with linguine.

INGREDIENTS:
- extra virgin olive oil
- 4-5 cloves garlic, minced
- 1 28 oz. can crushed tomatoes
- salt & pepper
- a pinch dried oregano
- 1 lb. shrimp, cleaned
- 1 lb. linguine pasta

DIRECTIONS:
1. Add a couple of drizzles oil to a large sauté pan. On medium heat, let the oil get hot and add the garlic. As it browns, add the tomatoes, salt & pepper to taste, and just a tiny pinch of dried oregano.
2. After about 10-15 minutes, add the shrimp and cook for about 5 minutes or until they turn pink.
3. While the sauce cooks, bring a large stockpot of water to boil, add salt to the boiling water, and cook pasta according to package instructions.
4. Drain the pasta, add the sauce, and combine. It's ready to plate and serve!

Sense & Sensibility – SALAD SENSIBILITY

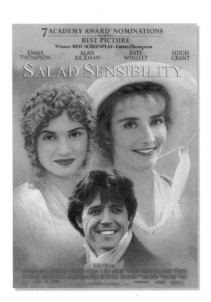

It's said that every good meal should include a sensible salad, hence the name.

INGREDIENTS:
- 1 head romaine lettuce
- 1 head radicchio
- 1 head endive
- 1 11 oz. can mandarin oranges, drained
- 1 oz. almonds, sliced
- creamy Italian salad dressing
- apple cider vinegar

DIRECTIONS:
1. Wash and pat dry the romaine, radicchio, and endive. "Rip" it into bite-sized pieces and put in a large bowl. Add mandarin oranges, raisins, and sliced almonds.
2. In a small bowl, add 2 tbsp. dressing with 2 tsp. vinegar and whisk.
3. Pour dressing over salad, combine well, and serve.

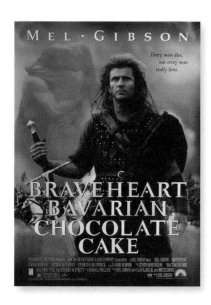

Braveheart – BRAVEHEART BAVARIAN CHOCOLATE CAKE

I didn't know what to do about this one so I went for a touch of alliteration and threw in the word "Bavarian" to imply superior chocolate. Using heart-shaped pans seemed obvious, as was the split white and blue frosting. Freeeeeeedom!

INGREDIENTS:

- 1/2 cup + 1 tbsp. vegetable oil
- 1 3/4 cup + 2 tbsp. flour
- 1 1/2 cup sugar
- 3/4 cup unsweetened cocoa
- 1 1/2 tsp. baking powder
- 1 1/2 tsp. baking soda
- 1 tsp. + 1/4 tsp. salt
- 2 large eggs
- 1 cup + 2 tbsp. milk

- 2 tsp. + 1 tsp. vanilla
- 1 cup water, boiling
- raspberries
- blueberries
- strawberries
- 4 tbsp. butter, softened
- 2 cup confectioners sugar
- blue food coloring

DIRECTIONS:

1. Preheat oven to 350°. Grease and flour 2 heart-shaped bake pans.
2. Combine flour, sugar, cocoa, baking powder, baking soda, and salt. Add in oil, eggs, milk, and vanilla. Beat for about 2 minutes. Stir in water – the batter will be thin. Pour evenly into both pans.
3. Bake for 30 minutes (or until tester comes out clean) and cool in pan for 10 minutes before transferring it to cooling rack.
4. For frosting, whisk butter, confectioners sugar, salt, milk, and vanilla. Split amount into separate bowls, add a few drops of blue food coloring to one and mix to create the blue color.
5. When cake is cool, place the first heart on a serving plate, add a layer of white frosting and scatter berries before adding the second heart. Frost the left side of the heart with blue frosting and the right side with white frosting. Garnish with berries and serve.

My personal party night food photo of "Braveheart Bavarian Chocolate Cake":

1997

The 69th Academy Awards®   **Host: Billy Crystal**
The Shrine Auditorium   **March 24, 1997**

And so began the year I started hosting for hosting's sake. I remember it was a tough group. I sat in the theater watching Shine after it was nominated hoping to be inspired for a dish. I was hard-pressed to think of the menu as the choices reflect. Everything was delicious but it was a random selection.

Fargo - FARGO SLUSHES

I loved this movie but there was nothing to inspire me in it. However there was cold and snow. So why not makes some cocktail slushes?

INGREDIENTS:
- sugar syrup
- lemon vodka, chilled
- 1 lemon's juice
- crushed ice

DIRECTIONS:
1. To create sugar syrup, you need 2 parts water to 1 part sugar. Bring water to a boil, dissolve sugar, stirring constantly. Remove from heat and cool.
2. Mix 1 1/2 oz. vodka, 3/4 oz. lemon juice, and 1 tsp. sugar syrup per serving needed with crushed ice.
3. Serve in a fancy glass!

Secrets & Lies – SECRET SAUCE & BOWTIES

The clients of my father's wholesale produce business were famous Manhattan restaurants and he counted the owners and chefs as good friends. I won't divulge where he became inspired for this one, even though the doors have been closed for years – because I can keep a secret.

INGREDIENTS:
- extra virgin olive oil
- 1 yellow onion, chopped
- 2 slices pancetta, chopped
- 1-2 oz. brandy
- 1 28 oz. can crushed tomatoes
- salt & pepper
- 1/2 cup heavy cream
- 1 lb. bowtie past

DIRECTIONS:
1. Drizzle oil into a large sauté pan, add onion on medium heat until translucent.
2. Pour in the brandy carefully – it may flame. The alcohol needs to burn out.
3. Add tomatoes, salt & pepper to taste. Stir in a bit of heavy cream so the color turns a medium pink. Cover. It will be ready in about 15 minutes.
4. While the sauce cooks, make pasta according to package instructions.
5. Drain the pasta, add the sauce, and combine. Plate and serve!

The English Patient – THE ENGLISH PEPPER

This is my grandfather Tony's recipe, which uses a breadcrumb stuffing, a nod to the sand from the desert scenes (did I say some of these would be a stretch? Ha!).

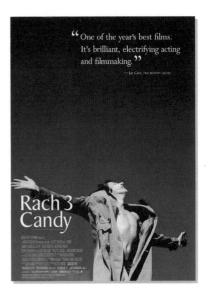

INGREDIENTS:
- 8-10 cloves garlic, minced
- 2 tsp. fresh or dried parsley
- 2 cups plain bread crumbs
- 1/2 cup grated Romano cheese
- 1 small tomato, diced
- salt & pepper
- extra virgin olive oil
- 4 cubanelle peppers, washed and cored

DIRECTIONS:
1. Mix garlic, parsley, bread crumbs, cheese, tomato, and salt & pepper to taste.
2. Add oil little by little until the bread crumb mixture is "wet" – stays together but isn't soggy.
3. Fill peppers up to an inch from the top.
4. In a large frying pan, add a generous amount of oil and heat. Hold up each pepper to fry the bottom before laying down to fry all sides. They're done when they get brownish and soften. Plate & serve!

Shine – RACH 3 CANDY

I was at a loss. The only thing I could think of was playing off (pun intended) the featured music piece that the main character needed to perform – Piano Concerto No. 3 in D minor by Rachmaninoff, referred to as Rach 3 – Rock candy.

INGREDIENTS:
- stirring sticks of rock candy, one per guest
- coffee

DIRECTIONS:
1. Prepare coffee as you normally would.
2. Add candy stick and use it to stir in the sugary sweetness.

Jerry Maguire – CHERRY MAGUIRE PIE

I took the easy way out when putting together this pie, sort of like Jerry's approach to love at the start of the movie. Ha!

INGREDIENTS:

- 1 box refrigerated pie crusts, room temperature
- 2 cans cherry pie filling

DIRECTIONS:

1. Preheat oven to 425°. Using a 9" pie plate, lay out 1 sheet of dough.
2. Pour in cherry pie filling.
3. Add second layer of dough, seal edges, and make slits in the top to let steam out. Bake about 40 minutes or until crust is golden. Check after about 20 minutes – if the crust is getting too brown, add a ring of foil to protect it from burning.
4. Let cool for about 30 minutes before eating. We couldn't resist serving it with Cherry Garcia Ice Cream.

My personal party night food photo of "Cherry Maguire Pie":

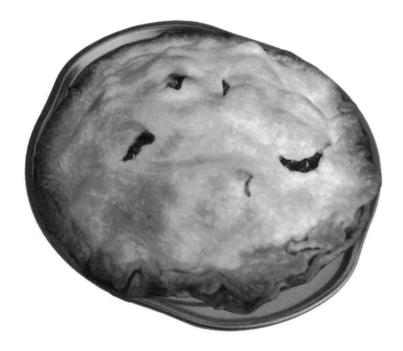

1998

The 70th Academy Awards®
The Shrine Auditorium

Host: Billy Crystal
March 23, 1998

This was the first year that I had each category properly designated. It was also the first year that the dishes weren't quite a stretch too. I was getting the hang of this!

As Good As It Gets – AS GOOEY AS IT GETS

You can't beat a delicious 9-layer dip with tortilla chips!

INGREDIENTS:

- 2 cans black beans, drained
- 1 cup monterey jack cheese, shredded
- 2 cups guacamole
- 1 red onion, chopped
- 16 oz. Greek yogurt
- 2 cups salsa
- 1 cup cheddar cheese, shredded
- 8 oz. black olives, pitted & sliced
- 3 tomatoes, diced
- 1 tsp. fresh cilantro, minced
- 1 large bag tortilla chips

DIRECTIONS:

1. Using a deep, clear bowl, loosely layer in beans, then cheese, guacamole, onion, yogurt, salsa, cheddar, black olives, and tomatoes & cilantro, combining tomatoes and cilantro for the final top layer.
2. Put out the chips and go for the gooey deliciousness!

L.A. Confidential – LASAGNA CONFIDENTIAL

That movie had layers, just like this lasagna! There are some steps to this – but it's easy and well worth it!!

INGREDIENTS:

- 2 lbs. curly lasagne pasta
- 3 lbs. ricotta
- 1/2 lb. grated Romano cheese
- 1 tbsp. fresh or dried parsley
- salt & pepper
- 4 large eggs
- extra virgin olive oil
- 1 yellow onion, diced
- 1 lb. chop meat
- 3 28 oz. cans crushed tomatoes
- fresh or dried basil
- 1 lb. mozzarella, sliced

DIRECTIONS:

1. Preheat oven to 325°. Prepare lasagne sheets according to package instructions. Rinse in cold water and set aside.
2. Heat a couple of drizzles of oil in a large sauté pan and add onions – cook until limp. Add chop meat and brown. Pour in tomatoes, basil to taste, salt & pepper to taste. Let cook about 30 minutes.
3. In a large bowl, combine ricotta, Romano, parsley, salt & pepper to taste, and eggs. Set aside.
4. Using a deep baking dish, you'll build in layers in the following order – a covering of meat sauce, lasagne, meat sauce, ricotta mix, mozzarella. Keep going until you get to the top of the dish and end with a covering of sauce.
5. Bake for 90 minutes. Let it set for about 30 minutes before you cut it and serve.

The Full Monty – THE FULL ARTI

The only rationale I can provide for using stuffed artichokes is that the blokes didn't "choke" when they took it all off!

INGREDIENTS:
- 2 cups seasoned bread crumbs
- 1/2 cup grated Romano cheese
- 4 cloves garlic, minced
- 2 tsp. dried parsley
- extra virgin olive oil
- 6 medium-sized artichokes

DIRECTIONS:
1. Using shears, snip the points of the artichoke leaves. Slice across the top so they have a flat top. As you wash them under water, press leaves open to make space between leaves.
2. In a bowl, mix bread crumbs, cheese, garlic, and parsley. Add oil little by little until the breadcrumb mixture is "wet" – stays together but isn't soggy.
3. Stuff artichoke leaves with bread crumb mixture – use spoon to really get it down in between the leaves.
4. Add about 1/2" water to the bottom of a large stockpot. Place the artichokes standing in the pot side-by-side.
5. On a low flame, cook until tender, about 30 minutes. Remove and serve.

Titanic – ICEBERG SALAD WITH ENDIVE

I don't want to be "cold" but she said she'd never let go but then she did and he sunk to the bottom. Yikes! I also could have called this a "Sail-ad" but that was pushing it.

INGREDIENTS:
- 1 head iceberg lettuce
- 1 head endive
- extra virgin olive oil
- white balsamic vinegar
- salt & pepper

DIRECTIONS:
1. Wash iceberg and endive. Rip into bite sized pieces.
2. Add 2 drizzles of oil, a drizzle of vinegar, and salt & pepper to taste.
3. Mix and serve!

Good Will Hunting – GOOD WILL BUNDT CAKE

It's a sweet Boston cream moment in a funny pan! Haaaa-vahd Yahd never had such a "good will" cake!

INGREDIENTS:

- 2 cup flour, sifted
- 2 tsp. baking powder
- 1/2 tsp. salt
- 4 large eggs, separated
- 1-1/2 cup sugar, divided
- 3/4 cup hot water
- 1 tsp. vanilla
- 8 oz. vanilla pudding, pre-made or mix prepared
- 15 oz. jar hot fudge

DIRECTIONS:

1. Preheat oven to 325°. Sift flour, baking powder, and salt.
2. In a separate bowl, beat egg whites until they form peaks.
3. In another bowl, beat egg yolks until they are thick. Add about half the sugar and continue beating. Add hot water and vanilla and remaining sugar. Beat thoroughly. Fold in egg whites, then flour mixture.
4. Pour into greased bundt pan. Bake 45-50 minutes or until tester comes out clean.
5. Cool for 10 minutes before removing from pan and place on cooling rack. When fully cooled, slice cake in half to create 2 layers.
6. Spread pudding over bottom layer and replace top layer.
7. Heat hot fudge and pour evenly around the top.

My personal party night food photos of "The Full Arti" and "LAsagne Confidential":

1999

The 71st Academy Awards®   Host: Whoopi Goldberg
The Dorothy Chandler Pavilion   March 21, 1999

The nominated movies were in two categories to me - "at war" and "the late 16th Century". The meals were geting more interesting to devise with a lot of creative help from friends and family.

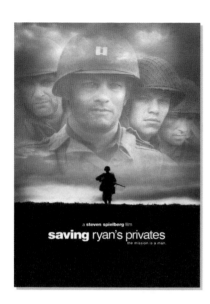

Saving Private Ryan – SAVING RYAN'S PRIVATES

This choice has nothing to do with that incredible movie and everything to do with a pleasingly snarky turn of a title by my good friend Anne Flynn.

INGREDIENTS:
- 1 100-ct package mini cocktail franks in puff pastry, frozen
- spicy brown mustard
- 2 lbs. "meatloaf mix" chop meat – veal, pork, beef
- 1/2 lb. Romano cheese
- 3 large eggs
- 6 cloves garlic, minced
- 1/2 lb. seasoned bread crumbs
- salt & pepper
- vegetable oil

DIRECTIONS:
1. Prepare mini cocktail franks according to package directions. Serve with mustard.
2. Mix chop meat, cheese, eggs, garlic, bread crumbs, and salt & pepper to taste. Form balls about 2" in diameter.
3. Pour oil in a deep frying pan about half way and heat on medium. When the oil is hot, add the meatballs. Turn to thoroughly cook on all sides and remove them to a paper lined dish to absorb excess oil. Plate and serve!

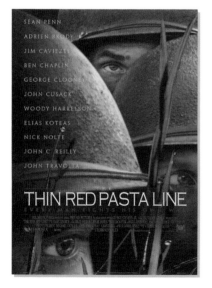

The Thin Red Line – THIN RED PASTA LINE

It's very thin angel hair pasta with an "explosive" spicy red tomato sauce!

INGREDIENTS:
- extra virgin olive oil
- 1 medium yellow onion, chopped
- 2 28 oz. cans crushed tomatoes
- fresh or dried basil
- salt & pepper
- red pepper flakes
- 1 lb. angel hair pasta
- grated Romano cheese

DIRECTIONS:
1. Heat a drizzle of oil in a large sauté pan, add onions – cook until translucent.
2. Pour in canned tomatoes, basil, salt, and pepper to taste. Add red pepper flakes to taste. Let cook about 30 minutes.
3. Cook pasta according to package instructions. Drain to bowl and ladle sauce on top. Sprinkle cheese on top as you like!

Shakespeare in Love – BAKED SPEARS YOU'LL LOVE

Ok, ok... a TOTAL stretch! But it is Shake-SPEAR-e! And "cheesy" like this romantic movie.

INGREDIENTS:
- 1 bunch large asparagus
- extra virgin olive oil
- 1/2 cup seasoned bread crumbs
- 1/2 cup shredded Parmesan cheese
- salt & pepper

DIRECTIONS:
1. Steam asparagus until they are softened but not limp.
2. Preheat oven to 350°. Place asparagus on a baking sheet and brush with olive oil. Liberally sprinkle bread crumbs and cheese. Add salt & pepper to taste.
3. Bake for about 10 minutes or until cheese melts and the bread crumbs brown. Plate and serve.

Life is Beautiful – LIFE IS BOUNTIFUL

Well life is beautiful AND bountiful. A salad is a proud display of a harvest so it's a perfect choice.

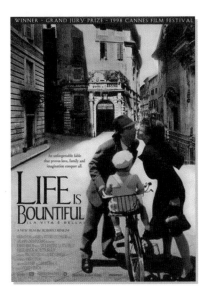

INGREDIENTS:
- 8 oz. pitted Kalamata olives
- 8 oz. roasted red peppers
- 8 oz. marinated artichokes
- 1 head green leaf lettuce, cleaned and chopped
- 1 head red leaf lettuce, cleaned and chopped
- extra virgin olive oil
- white balsamic vinegar
- salt & pepper

DIRECTIONS:
1. In a large bowl, combine olives, peppers, artichokes, and lettuces. Drizzle olive oil liberally. Follow with half that amount of vinegar. Add salt & pepper to taste. Mix well and serve.

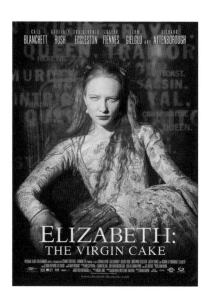

Elizabeth: The Virgin Queen - ELIZABETH: THE VIRGIN CAKE

It's a purely delicious cake with white frosting.

INGREDIENTS:

- 2 cups flour, sifted
- 2 tsp. baking powder
- 1/2 tsp. salt
- 1 cup butter, divided
- 1 cup sugar
- 2 large eggs, beaten
- 2 tsp. vanilla, divided
- 1/2 cup + 2 tbsp. milk
- 2 cups confectioners sugar
- raspberries

DIRECTIONS:

1. Preheat oven to 375°. Sift flour, baking powder, and salt twice.
2. In a separate large bowl, cream together 1/2 cup butter, sugar, and 1 tsp. vanilla until soft and fluffy.
3. Add eggs and beat well.
4. Add a bit of flour, then 1/2 cup milk alternating until it's all well blended.
5. Grease 2 9" layer pans and pour in the batter. Bake for about 25 minutes or until tester comes out clean. Cool thoroughly.
6. Whisk remaining butter, vanilla, and milk with confectioners sugar.
7. Plate one cake layer and add frosting before adding second layer. Frost top and sides of cake. Add raspberries to garnish the top. Slice and enjoy!

My personal party night food photo of "Baked Spears You'll Love":

2000

The 72nd Academy Awards®   **Host: Billy Crystal**
The Shrine Auditorium   **March 26, 2000**

It was a new century! New awards! New posters!
This was the first year I attempted to create posters
to complement the food. Prior to this year, I had the
names printed and cut out to place on the dishes.
Yes, I went back to create those years of posters
for this book.

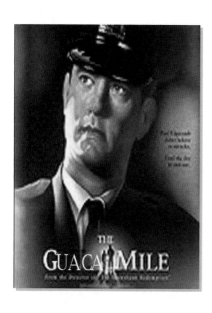

The Green Mile – THE GUACA MILE

A long dish of freshly made guacamole, captured on a crunchy chip, can electrify your taste buds!

INGREDIENTS:

- 6 avocados
- 1 red onion, diced
- 1 jalapeño pepper, diced
- 2 plum tomatoes, diced
- 2 tsp. fresh cilantro, washed and chopped
- juice from 2 Limes
- sea salt & black pepper, freshly ground
- 1 bag tortilla chips

DIRECTIONS:

1. Cut avocado vertically around the pit – ease avocado apart. Scoop out avocado "meat" and place in a bowl.
2. Add onion, pepper, tomatoes, cilantro, lime juice, and salt & pepper to taste.
3. Coarsely mash together until avocado is mostly smooth with some chunks.
4. Serve with chip
5. s on a long narrow plate.

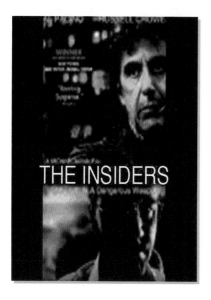

The Insider – THE INSIDERS

What's better than two varieties of pizza dough with amazing flavors inside? In this case pepperoni in one and spinach rolled inside the other.

INGREDIENTS:

- extra virgin olive oil
- 2 cloves garlic, minced
- 1 package spinach, frozen chopped and thawed
- salt & pepper
- 2 lbs. pizza dough, fresh or refrigerated, divided, at room temperature
- 1/2 lb. muenster cheese, very thinly sliced
- 1/4 lb. pepperoni, very thinly sliced

DIRECTIONS:

1. Preheat oven to 400°. Roll out dough into two circles as large as they will go.
2. Using a sauté pan, add olive oil and on medium heat, cook garlic until it begins to brown. Add spinach, salt & pepper to taste and cook for about 10 minutes.
3. Layer each dough circle with cheese slices. Add pepperoni slices to one and spinach to the other. Roll up thin, fold over the ends so there's no gap.
4. Place each roll on a cookie sheet. Bake for 30 minutes until they are golden brown and crusty good. Remove from oven, let cool. Slice and serve warm.

American Beauty – AMERICAN BOOTY

An all-American "rump" roast is always a dish of beauty!

INGREDIENTS:

- extra virgin olive oil
- 3 lbs. bottom round/rump roast
- 2 yellow onions, quartered & sliced
- 2 cups beef bouillon/broth/stock
- salt & pepper
- 1 lb. egg noodles

DIRECTIONS:

1. In a deep pot on low heat, add a couple of drizzles of olive oil.
2. Add meat "fat side" down. With heat raised to medium, sear on all sides — remove from pot. Set aside.
3. Add sliced onions to the pot with salt & pepper to taste, and brown.
4. Stir in bouillon/broth then put meat back in the pot and cover — lower heat.
5. After 30 minutes, stir and continue to cook until meat is well done, likely another 60-90 minutes. Remove meat from pot and slice.
6. Prepare noodles according to package instructions. Drain, place in a bowl, and stir in some of the onion jus.
7. Serve the pot roast on a bed of noodles with onion jus.

The Sixth Sense – THE SIX SENSIBLES

I morbidly thought if you eat sensibly, you don't have to worry about being dead and not know it. Of course you'll have to have seen the movie to "get that". Heh heh.

INGREDIENTS:

- 1 head radicchio, washed and chopped
- 1 head romaine, washed and chopped
- 1 bulb fennel, cut into bite-sized chunks
- mache, washed
- walnuts, chopped
- 1/2 cup cheddar cheese, shredded
- salt & pepper
- 1/2 cup extra virgin olive oil
- 1/4 cup apple cider vinegar

DIRECTIONS:

1. In a large bowl, combine radicchio, romaine, fennel, mache, walnuts, and cheese. Add salt & pepper to taste.
2. Pour in olive oil and vinegar and mix well. Serve!

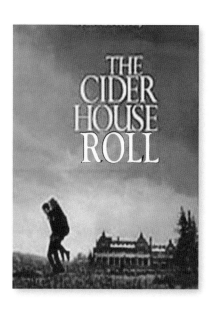

The Cider House Rules – THE CIDER HOUSE ROLL

One of my favorite desserts has been the Apple Horn from Enrico's Pastries on Morris Park Avenue in the Bronx. Since it's roll-shaped, it's just what the doctor ordered! I adopted it as this year's dessert.

INGREDIENTS:

* apple strudel-type cake from local bakery or market

DIRECTIONS:
1. Purchase the cake.
2. Slice and serve!

My personal party night food photos of "American Booty" and "The Guacamile":

2001

The 73rd Academy Awards®   **Host: Steve Martin**
The Shrine Auditorium   **March 25, 2001**

The reputation for my Oscar® gatherings had grown
but my little apartment was bursting at the seams.
My sister Nancy agreed to host at her larger place.
The layout was much better for hosting!

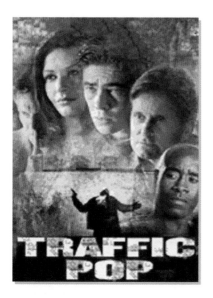

Traffic – TRAFFIC POP & TRAFFICANA

This was the only time one movie got two different selections – an appetizer and a cocktail. I reasoned that after eating Jalapeño Poppers, Vodka and OJ is good.

INGREDIENTS:
- vodka, chilled
- orange juice
- 1 50-ct. jalapeño poppers
- ranch salad dressing

DIRECTIONS:
1. Mix 1 1/2 oz. vodka and 3 oz. orange juice per serving. Pour over ice.
2. Prepare according to package instructions.
3. Dip in ranch dressing.

Crouching Tiger Hidden Dragon – CROUCHING TIGER PRAWN HIDDEN DRAGON STEAK

A glorious movie and the perfect excuse for a delicious stir fry!

INGREDIENTS:
- 1/3 cup teriyaki sauce
- 3 tbsp. brown sugar
- 1 tsp. corn starch
- salt
- 1 lb. steak, sliced
- 1 lb. shrimp, cleaned
- 3/4 cup vegetable oil, divided
- 2 cloves garlic, minced
- 1/2 tsp. ground ginger, divided
- 1 red bell pepper, sliced
- 1 green bell pepper, sliced
- 1 yellow bell pepper, sliced
- 1 medium yellow onion, sliced
- 1/4 lb. mushrooms, cleaned and sliced
- 1/2 tsp. red pepper flakes
- 1 cup rice, cooked

DIRECTIONS:
1. In a large bowl, mix teriyaki sauce, brown sugar, corn starch, and salt. Add steak and shrimp to marinate.
2. Heat 1/4 cup oil in wok or large skillet. Add steak and stir fry for about 5 minutes. Drain meat, reserve juices, and set aside. Wipe out pan.
3. Heat another 1/4 cup oil in pan. Add garlic, half the ginger, peppers, meat and shrimp. Stir fry for 2-4 minutes, drain, and set it aside. Wipe out pan.
4. Add remaining 1/4 cup oil to the pan and the rest of the ginger with the onions. Stir fry for 3 minutes and add the mushrooms, peppers, and red pepper flakes to taste. After another minute, add back in the meat, shrimp, peppers, and remaining marinade. Stir fry until it's all to desired doneness. Serve over rice.

**Erin Brockovich: Based on a True Story –
ERIN BROCCOLI: BASED ON A TRUE STALK**

This is a stand-out, go-to recipe for broccoli that you'll make over and over. Dipping the bread into the tart oily juices with a bite of broccoli elevates the simple stalks!

INGREDIENTS:
- 1 head broccoli, cleaned and cut into strips
- 4 cloves garlic, chopped
- 1/4 cup extra virgin olive oil
- juice of 1 lemon
- 1 loaf crusty Italian bread

DIRECTIONS:
1. Steam broccoli to desired tenderness. Place on plate.
2. In a separate small bowl, mix garlic, olive oil, and lemon juice. Pour over the broccoli and serve with bread for dipping.

Gladiator – SALADIATOR

Be a salad warrior with this rich and delicious dish!

INGREDIENTS:
- 1 head romaine, cleaned
- 3 oz. dry sundried tomatoes
- 1/2 lb. ricotta salata cheese
- extra virgin olive oil
- red wine vinegar
- 2 tbsp. grated Romano cheese
- 1 clove garlic, minced
- salt & pepper

DIRECTIONS:
1. Rip romaine into bite-sized pieces and place in a large bowl. Add in sundried tomatoes and crumble in ricotta salata cheese.
2. In a small dish, whisk together olive oil, vinegar, grated cheese, garlic, and salt & pepper to taste.
3. Pour dressing over salad and mix well. Plate and serve!

Chocolat – CHOCOLAT TREATS

Never has there been an easier menu selection! But so many choices... In order not to "fudge" it, I picked fudge!

INGREDIENTS:
- 2 cups sugar
- 1/2 cup unsweetened cocoa
- 1 cup milk
- 1/4 tsp. salt
- small dish of Ice water
- 4 tbsp. + 1 tbsp. butter
- 1 tsp. vanilla

DIRECTIONS:
1. Whisk sugar, cocoa, milk, and salt in a medium pot. Then bring to stove and on medium heat, keep stirring, bring to a boil. Reduce heat to as low as you can while it still bubbles, stirring very little.
2. If you want to use a candy thermometer, cook until it gets to about 235°. I don't. Instead, cook a bit 'til you see the bubbles getting smaller and drizzle a bit into a small dish of ice water and see if it forms a soft squishy ball. If it does, it's done.
3. Remove from heat. Stir in 4 tbsp. butter and vanilla. Beat until the fudge starts to cool but isn't thick.
4. Butter an 8" pan and pour fudge in. Let it cool well for at least 30 minutes. Cut into bite-sized squares and savor.

My personal party night food photo of "Erin Broccoli: Based on a True Stalk":

2002

The 74th Academy Awards®   Host: Whoopi Goldberg
The Dolby Theater   March 24, 2002

The year before was such a success at "Chez Nancy", that she agreed to let me take over her apartment again! The party got a bit boisterous so, suffice to say, this was the final adventure at Nancy's. I will always appreciate her offer to take on the "Oscar® Insanity"!

**Lord of the Rings: The Fellowship of the Ring –
THE SWORD IN THE SPRINGS: THE FILLING IS FROM BEIJING**

This began three years of Lord of the Rings movies – difficult! They're great flicks, but making menu selections from them… not so great. I pulled a lazy move again with this. Humor me!

INGREDIENTS:
- telephone number of great local Chinese restaurant that delivers
- telephone
- sword-shaped plastic toothpicks

DIRECTIONS:
1. Call the restaurant to order the spring rolls.
2. Pay the delivery person when they arrive and tip well.
3. Transfer to plate, spear each roll with a toothpick, and serve!

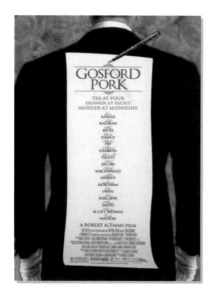

Gosford Park – GOSFORD PORK

A proper pork roast for a proper British manor home!

INGREDIENTS:
- 5 lbs. loin of pork roast
- extra virgin olive oil
- salt & pepper

DIRECTIONS:
1. Preheat the oven to 350°.
2. Place meat in roasting pan and rub with olive oil then season with salt & pepper to taste.
3. Cover with foil for about 20 minutes then take off. Roast for 1 hour 40 minutes or until center temperature reaches 145°. Let rest 15 minutes and serve.

In The Bedroom – IN THE MUSHROOM

It was a perfect complement to the roast and worked with the title. I love a good stuffed mushroom.

INGREDIENTS:
- 2 cups seasoned bread crumbs
- 1/2 cup grated Romano cheese
- 3 tbsp. fresh parsley, stemmed and chopped
- extra virgin olive oil
- 2 lbs. white mushrooms for stuffing, cleaned and stemmed

DIRECTIONS:
1. Preheat oven to 400°.
2. In a bowl, mix bread crumbs, cheese, and parsley. Add oil little by little until the breadcrumb mixture is "wet" – stays together but isn't soggy.
3. Place mushrooms in a baking pan. Bake for 25 minutes or until tops are browned. Take from the oven, plate, and serve.

A Beautiful Mind – A BLEU-TIFUL HEAD

It didn't occur to me until later that I didn't use a head of lettuce! Of course you can, but the delicate mesclun with the robust dressing was a perfect match.

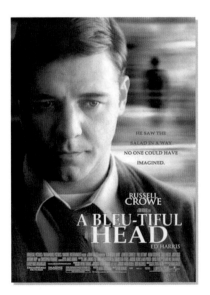

INGREDIENTS:
- 16 oz. sour cream
- 4 oz. mayonnaise
- 2 oz. white vinegar
- salt & pepper
- 1/4 lb. bleu cheese, crumbled
- 16 oz. mesclun/spring mix lettuce, rinsed

DIRECTIONS:
1. In a small bowl, whisk sour cream, mayonnaise, vinegar, and salt & pepper to taste. Toss in the blue cheese and mix.
2. Place mesclun in large bowl and drizzle dressing over it. Mix well and serve.

Moulin Rouge – MOULIN ROUGE TART

I saw this movie at the famous Ziegfeld Theater in Manhattan. It has a stage with a grand red curtain. As the movie began, the curtains opened. And I recall the movie starts with red curtains opening too. It was a grand spectacle, amazing color and music... I loved it and can still be caught singing those inspired mash-ups. This dish is an homage to Satine, the courtesan... or tart!

INGREDIENTS:

- 2 cups flour
- 1 pinch salt
- 1/3 cup brown sugar
- 1 stick plus 3 tbsp. unsalted butter, chilled & diced
- 2 large egg yolks, lightly beaten
- 2 pints raspberries
- 1/4 cup sugar
- 1 tbsp. corn starch
- 1 tbsp. water

DIRECTIONS:

1. Preheat oven to 350°. Combine flour, salt, and brown sugar. Mix in butter until coarse. Add egg yolks and blend well as it forms into a dough.
2. Using a 9" tart pan with removable bottom, press dough into the bottom and a 1/2" up the sides evenly. Bake 25-30 minutes until light brown. Remove to cooling rack.
3. Place 3/4 of the raspberries and sugar in a saucepan. Cook over medium heat until it boils.
4. Separately, stir cornstarch with 1 tbsp. water then add to raspberry mixture. Cook about 3 minutes, stirring until mixture thickens slightly, then remove from heat. Let cool.
5. Remove rim of tart pan and pour raspberry mixture into tart shell. Cover with plastic wrap and refrigerate until set.
6. When it's ready, garnish with remaining raspberries and indulge.

My personal party night food photos of "In The Mushroom" and "Gosford Pork":

2003

The 75th Academy Awards®   **Host: Steve Martin**
The Dolby Theater   **March 23, 2003**

This was the first Oscar® celebration held at my brand new apartment at the time. The space was definitely better than before. The show was great and the food... well... ya know... FABULOUS!

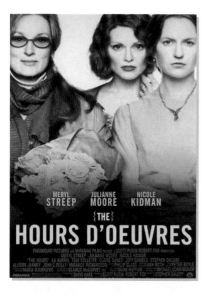

The Hours – THE HOURS D'OEUVRES

I certainly did a play-on-words here. And I hate to report, but I did a variety of frozen appetizers again! I know, I know... not inspired. But I did choose puff pastry ones this time. So here's the same ol' "recipe".

INGREDIENTS:
- 1 package 100-ct. mixed hors d'oeuvres, frozen

DIRECTIONS:
1. Prepare according to package instructions and serve.

Chicago – CHICAGO PIZZA

Chicago is a great town. As a New Yorker, I'm partial to our thin-crust style. However, my grandfather always made a deep dish "Sicilian-style" pizza. My mom still makes it almost every Friday night! It's my version of Chicago deep dish pizza.

INGREDIENTS:
- 16 oz. plain tomato sauce
- 1 medium yellow onion, diced
- extra virgin olive oil
- salt & pepper
- 2 lbs. pizza dough, fresh or frozen, room temperature
- 16 oz. packaged mozzarella, shredded
- 1 lb. freshly grated Romano cheese

DIRECTIONS:
1. Preheat oven to 400°. Drizzle olive oil in saucepan on medium heat, add onions and cook until translucent. Add tomato sauce and salt & pepper to taste. Stir, cover, & simmer for about 15 minutes.
2. Using an edged pan, spread out the dough, cover it and let it rise in a cool, dark place for an hour.
3. Add a light drizzle of oil in the bottom of pan, then spread out the dough. Spread shredded mozzarella liberally and evenly over the dough. Ladle tomato sauce evenly, finish with liberal amounts of grated cheese.
4. Bake for 30 minutes or until crust is golden brown and oozing cheesy goodness.

Gangs of New York – TANGS OF NEW PORK

A tangy sweet flavor for a "new pork" roast was an easy and delicious choice for the main course. I wouldn't endorse a name brand product – I tried to recreate the sweet peach-apricot glaze but there's just no comparing to Saucy Susan.

INGREDIENTS:
- 5 lbs. loin of pork roast
- 9.5 oz. Saucy Susan peach apricot glaze
- salt & pepper

DIRECTIONS:
1. Preheat the oven to 350°.
2. Place meat in roasting pan. Liberally spread it with Saucy Susan and season with salt & pepper to taste.
3. Cover with foil for about 20 minutes then take off. Roast for 1 hour 40 minutes or until center temperature reaches 145°. Let rest 15 minutes and serve.

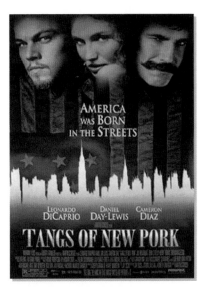

The Pianist – THE PEAS 'N' BLISS

Such a stretch, but a great side dish.

INGREDIENTS:
- 5 lbs. red bliss potatoes, washed and quartered
- 16 oz. peas, frozen and thawed
- 1 medium yellow onion, sliced
- extra virgin olive oil
- salt & pepper

DIRECTIONS:
1. Parboil (boil partially) potatoes for about 5 minutes and set aside.
2. In a large skillet, drizzle olive oil and on medium heat, sauté the onions until they are translucent. Add a couple more drizzles of olive oil, potatoes, and salt & pepper to taste.
3. After about 10 minutes, add peas and stir all together. Lower heat and cover. Let cook for another 10 minutes or until the potatoes are tender. Remove from heat, plate and serve.

**The Lord of the Rings: The Two Towers –
THE TORTE IN A RING: WITH NO FLOUR**

The second Lord of the Rings movie proved as much of a challenge as the first. But I ran "rings" around it! And yeah... a little flour (shhhh).

INGREDIENTS:

- 3/4 cup + 2 tbsp. butter
- 8 tbsp. unsweetened cocoa
- 1 cup sugar, divided
- 2 tbsp. flour
- 3 large eggs, separated
- 4 tbsp. water
- 1/2 tsp. vanilla
- 1 cup + 1/4 cup confectioners sugar
- 1 tbsp. milk
- yellow food coloring

DIRECTIONS:

1. Preheat oven to 350°. Melt 3/4 cup butter in pan over low heat.
2. Slowly stir in 6 tbsp. cocoa and 3/4 cup sugar until smooth. Let cool for 5 minutes. Blend in flour. Add egg yolks one at a time, then 2 tbsp. water.
3. In a separate bowl, combine remaining sugar and egg whites. Beat until soft peaks form. Fold into chocolate mixture.
4. Pour into a greased and floured 9" round layer pan. Bake for 30 minutes or until tester comes out clean. Cool for 10 minutes before turning out of pan to cooling rack.
5. To create glaze, melt 2 tbsp. butter in a pan over low heat. Add 2 tbsp. each cocoa and water and stir until it thickens – do not boil. Remove from heat and add vanilla. Whisk in 1 cup confectioners sugar until smooth. Spread on cake.
6. Stir milk, 1/4 cup confectioners sugar, and 3-4 drops yellow food coloring. Pipe around edge of cake to create golden ring. It's ready to serve.

My personal party night food photos of "Chicago Pizza" and "The Torte in a Ring: With No Flour":

2004

The 76th Academy Awards®   **Host: Billy Crystal**
The Dolby Theater   **February 29, 2004**

This meal took on a decidedly delicious New York
Jewish cultural flair what with latkes and brisket.
Oy vey – it was such a yummy day!

Mystic River – MYSTERY SLIVERS

I know, you're waiting for the usual "frozen appetizers" declaration. Not this time. Is it a mozzarella or zucchini stick? Ahhhh... mystery!

INGREDIENTS:
- 1 cup flour
- 2 large eggs, beaten
- 1 cup seasoned bread crumbs
- 1/4 cup grated Parmesan cheese
- 16 oz. packaged mozzarella, sliced into sticks
- 3 large zucchini, sliced lengthwise into sticks then halved
- vegetable oil

DIRECTIONS:
1. In one dish, mix bread crumbs & cheese. In separate dishes have flour and eggs.
2. Pour about 1/2-1" oil in skillet and heat.
3. Dredge mozzarella and zucchini sticks in flour, then eggs (letting excess drip
4. back into the bowl), then carefully put in the oil. Fry for about 3 minutes letting them get golden brown. Remove to paper-towel covered dish to absorb excess oil. Repeat until all the sticks are fried and dig right in!

Seabiscuit – SEEBRISKET

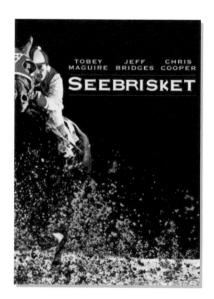

The obvious "biscuit" was in the race but lost by a nose. Brisket worked perfectly.

INGREDIENTS:
- extra virgin olive oil
- 3 lbs. beef brisket, trimmed
- 1 lb. carrots, peeled & chopped
- 1 head celery, washed and chopped
- 2 medium yellow onions, sliced
- salt & pepper

DIRECTIONS:
1. Preheat oven to 325°.
2. Add olive oil to a skillet and sear the meat on all sides.
3. Place in baking dish surrounded by carrots, celery, and onions. Season with salt & pepper to taste. Add about 1/4" water. Cover with foil and cook for 2-1/2 hours. Take foil off and cook for 30 minutes more.
4. Remove from oven, let rest for 15 minutes before slicing and plating with vegetables. Serve.

Lost in Translation – LATKE IN TRANSLATION

There is something about a crusty potato latke that NEVER gets lost in translation.

INGREDIENTS:
- 2 lbs. potatoes, peeled
- 1 small yellow onion
- 2 large eggs, beaten
- 2 tbsp. matzo meal
- salt & pepper
- vegetable oil
- 16 oz. apple sauce
- 16 oz. sour cream

DIRECTIONS:
1. Grate or shred potatoes. Place in a large bowl. Grate or shred onion and place in the same bowl. Add eggs and matzo meal, salt & pepper to taste.
2. Pour oil in a skillet. Heat on medium until oil is hot. Using a tablespoon, drop potato mixture carefully into the oil. Fry and turn over until golden brown – about 3 minutes. Place on paper towels to drain excess oil. Repeat until it's all fried.
3. Garnish with apple sauce and sour cream to serve.

Master & Commander: The Far Side of the World – MESCLUN & CUCUMBER: THE FRESH SIDE OF THE SALAD

A refreshing salad is just what this menu needed!

INGREDIENTS:
- 16 oz. Greek yogurt or sour cream
- 1 tbsp. fresh dill, chopped
- 1 tsp. sugar
- salt & pepper
- 16 oz. mesclun/spring mix, rinsed
- 3 cucumbers, peeled & sliced

DIRECTIONS:
1. Mix yogurt with dill, sugar, and salt & pepper to taste.
2. Add mesclun and cucumbers to a large bowl. Add yogurt dressing and mix. Plate and serve.

**The Lord of the Rings: The Return of the King –
THE SEARCH FOR THE RING: THE CAKE IS THE KING**

The final Lord of the Rings movie! I baked a Mardi Gras-style King's cake including baked-in trinket, since it was just a few days past. The tradition is that whomever gets the trinket must provide next year's King's cake. Hey... where's my cake? Ha!

INGREDIENTS:

- 4 tbsp. cinnamon
- 1 cup sugar
- 2 tbsp. flour (for rolling)
- 1 lbs. pizza dough
- 1 stick butter, melted
- 1 large egg, beaten

- 2 cups confectioners sugar
- 2 tbsp. milk
- green food coloring
- yellow food coloring
- red food coloring
- blue food coloring

DIRECTIONS:

1. Preheat oven to 375°. In a small bowl, combine cinnamon & sugar. Set aside.
2. Sprinkle flour on rolling surface. Roll out dough and liberally brush with butter.
3. Evenly distribute cinnamon sugar mixture over the buttery dough. If you're going to add a small trinket, now is the time – make sure it's thoroughly clean and is heat resistant and non-toxic.
4. Roll up and form into a ring shape, joining the ends. Brush egg wash over the top and bake for 30 minutes or until it becomes golden brown. Remove from the oven and let sit while you create the icing.
5. Whisk confectioners sugar and milk to create icing and separate into 3 smaller bowls to create the colors of Mardi Gras, green, yellow, and purple. To one bowl, add 3-4 green coloring drops and stir. To the next, add 3-4 drops yellow coloring and stir. To create purple, use 2 drops red and 2 drops blue– adjust as needed – and stir.
6. Drizzle the cake with the 3 colors in any way you like. Serve warm and see who gets the trinket!

My personal party night food photos of "Latke in Translation" and "Mesclun & Cucumber: The Fresh Side of the Salad":

2005

The 77th Academy Awards®   **Host: Chris Rock**
The Dolby Theater   **February 25, 2005**

What a year! Having Chris Rock host was a big deal.
He was tapped to bring in more youth to the audience
and freshen it up. I liked his acerbic jokes that made
digs at the actors and the show. The best joke being to
mock what he was honored to be a part of. The joke
was lost on the Academy – he wasn't asked back.

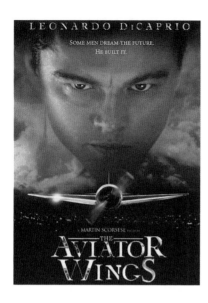

The Aviator – AVIATOR WINGS

This was a bit of a stretch but a delicious way for the meal to "take off"! Everyone loves Buffalo chicken wings.

INGREDIENTS:
- 20 chicken wings
- vegetable oil
- 2 tbsp. butter
- 1 cup hot sauce
- 6 stalks celery, cleaned and cut into small sticks
- 1 lb. carrots, peeled, cleaned, and cut into small sticks
- blue cheese dressing (see A Bleu-tiful Head in Chapter 8)

DIRECTIONS:
1. Add oil to large frying pan and heat on medium.
2. Fry the chicken wings and remove to a paper towel-lined plate to absorb excess oil.
3. Place chicken wings in a large bowl with butter and hot sauce. Combine until butter melts and the wings are evenly coated.
4. Serve with celery, carrots, and blue cheese dressing.

Finding Neverland – FINDING NEVERLAMB

A magical movie deserved a magical, aromatic dish. I left much of the chop's "handle" untrimmed – just enough off to hold easily.

INGREDIENTS:
- extra virgin olive oil
- 2 tsp. French lavender dried blossoms for cooking
- salt & pepper
- 20 lamb chops

DIRECTIONS:
1. Combine oil, lavender, and salt & pepper to taste in a large bowl. Add lamb chops and coat well, letting them marinate.
2. In a large grill pan, drizzle some olive oil and get it hot. On medium heat, add lamb, cooking about 3-5 minutes on each side, until they become crusty and brown – the center should be slightly rare but cook to your desired doneness.
3. Remove to paper towels to absorb the oil, plate and serve!

Million Dollar Baby – MILLION DOLLAR BLACK EYED PEAS

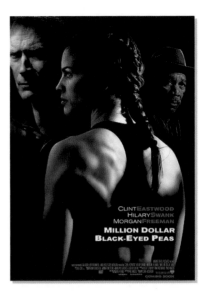

I had a little joke to myself about this one... humor me. Since it is a boxing movie, the black eyed peas were a fun choice. But peas... peace... opposite of fighting... are you with me? That was not lost on the group.

INGREDIENTS:
- extra virgin olive oil
- 1 small yellow onion, diced
- 4 slices bacon
- 15.5 oz. can black eyed peas
- salt & pepper

DIRECTIONS:
1. Drizzle olive oil in a skillet and, on medium heat, cook onions until soft.
2. Cut bacon into several pieces and add to the skillet. After a couple of minutes, add the peas. Season with salt & pepper to taste.
3. When the peas are heated through, plate and serve.

Sideways – SIDEGREENS

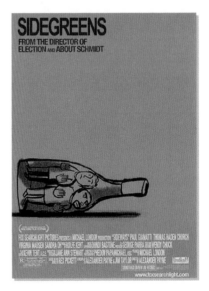

A movie where wine is a major character deserves a little wine in the salad! Red wine vinegar, that is...

INGREDIENTS:
- 1 head romaine, washed
- 1 head iceberg, washed
- 1 head radicchio, washed
- 2 cloves garlic, chopped
- salt & pepper
- extra virgin olive oil
- red wine vinegar

DIRECTIONS:
1. Chop romaine, iceberg, and radicchio into bite-sized pieces. Place with garlic into large bowl.
2. Season with salt & pepper to taste.
3. Add about 3-4 drizzles of olive oil followed by an equal amount of vinegar. Mix thoroughly and serve.

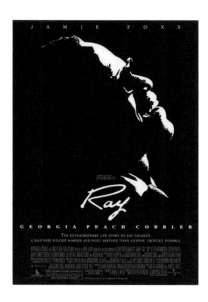

Ray – RAY GEORGIA PEACH COBBLER

To honor one of his most famous songs, Georgia On My Mind, I selected a sweet treat. I met Ray once in Newport, Rhode Island as he headed to his performance at Fort Adams State Park. What a nice man.

INGREDIENTS:
- 1 cup flour
- 2 cups sugar, divided
- 2 tsp. baking powder
- 1 pinch salt
- 1 cup milk
- 4 cups or about 6 peaches, peeled and sliced
- 1 tbsp. lemon juice
- 1 stick butter, melted
- 1/4 tsp. cinnamon

DIRECTIONS:
1. Preheat oven to 375°.
2. Combine flour, 1 cup sugar, baking powder, and salt in a bowl. Stir in milk until it's wet but not smooth.
3. Pour melted butter in rectangular baking dish followed by the batter but don't mix them together.
4. In a saucepan, add peaches, lemon juice, remaining sugar, and cinnamon, stirring constantly until boiling. Carefully pour the peach mixture over the batter and don't mix these in either.
5. Bake for about 40 minutes until the top is golden goodness. Serve warm but also good at room temperature.

My personal party night food photos of "Aviator Wings" and Finding Neverlamb":

2006

The 78th Academy Awards®
The Dolby Theater

Host: Jon Stewart
March 5, 2006

It was a great choice having Jon Stewart host. Being the Daily Show anchorman, his commentary was from a "media-like" perspective. A really fun show.

Brokeback Mountain – BROKEBACK MOUNTAIN OF RIBS

This recipe is so easy and flavorful. Most recipes call for adding a BBQ sauce but it diminishes the fabulous rub. Using honey gives the meat such great flavor and lets the rub really sing. You won't be able to quit it!

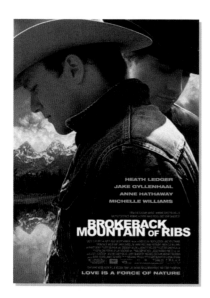

INGREDIENTS:

- 1 tbsp. ground black pepper
- 2 tsp. brown sugar
- 2 tsp. cayenne pepper
- 2 tsp. chili powder
- 2 tsp. ground cumin
- 1 tbsp. paprika
- 2 tsp. salt
- 1/2 tsp. sugar
- 1 lb. boneless baby back ribs, room temperature
- honey

DIRECTIONS:

1. Preheat oven to 400°. Lay a piece of foil on an edged baking sheet.
2. Combine black pepper, brown sugar, cayenne pepper, chili powder, cumin, paprika, salt, and sugar.
3. Place meat on the foil and rub spices liberally all over the meat on both sides. Seal in the foil and bake for 1 hour.
4. Remove from the oven, open the foil and spread honey on both sides of the meat. Leave foil open and place in the oven for another 15-20 minutes.
5. Feel free to add more honey as you like and savor the flavor!

Good Night & Good Luck – GOOD BITE OF GOOD CHUCK

Bite-sized burgers are all the rage. They're easy to make and so satisfying.

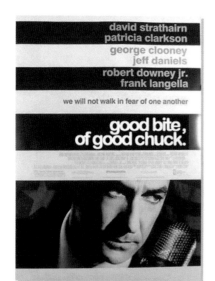

INGREDIENTS:

- 2 lbs. ground chuck
- 2 cloves garlic, minced
- 1/2 cup grated Romano cheese
- fresh parsley, minced
- 2 large eggs
- 1/2 cup plain bread crumbs
- salt & pepper
- package of small rolls

DIRECTIONS:

1. In a large bowl, mix meat, garlic, cheese, parsley, eggs, bread crumbs, and salt & pepper to taste. Shape into about 16 patties.
2. Heat a large grill pan and grill patties about 3 minutes on each side or until cooked to desired doneness.
3. Toast rolls, place a patty on each roll and serve.

Crash – CRASH'D POTATOES

There are well-blended mashed potatoes and then there are rough & tumble potatoes crashed together in a palate pleasing pile – so good!

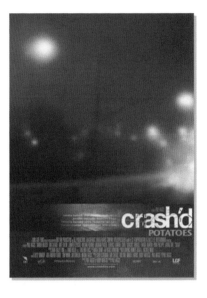

INGREDIENTS:
- 2 lbs. unpeeled potatoes, cleaned and cubed
- 1/4 cup milk
- 1/2 cup butter
- 2 tbsp. Greek yogurt
- 2 tsp. garlic, minced
- 2 tsp. fresh parsley
- 1/2 tsp. cayenne pepper
- salt & pepper

DIRECTIONS:
1. Boil potatoes in large stockpot until they are softened, about 10-15 minutes. Drain well and put in large bowl.
2. Add milk, butter, and yogurt – mash to desired texture.
3. Mix in garlic, parsley, cayenne pepper, and salt & pepper to taste.

Munich – MUNCH IT

A crunchy salad really makes the meal!

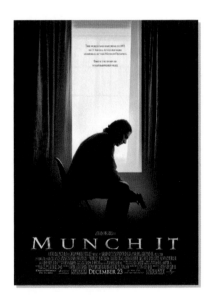

INGREDIENTS:
- 1 bulb fennel
- 4 stalks celery,
- 1 yellow pepper
- 1 red pepper
- 1 head iceberg
- 1/4 cup almonds, sliced
- extra virgin olive oil
- white vinegar
- salt & pepper

DIRECTIONS:
1. Chop fennel, celery, peppers, and iceberg and put in a large bowl. Add almonds.
2. Drizzle in a generous amount of olive oil and vinegar, salt, and pepper to taste. Mix well and serve.

Capote – FRUIT COMPOTE CHEESECAKE

Truman Capote was an interesting, talented man. I don't think he would be referred to as sweet, but he certainly enjoyed indulgences, like cheesecake!

INGREDIENTS:
- 1-1/2 cups graham cracker crumbs
- 1/4 cup butter, melted
- 1 cup + 1/4 cup sugar
- 3/4 tsp. salt, divided
- 16 oz. cream cheese, room temperature
- 2 large eggs
- 2 tsp. vanilla
- 1 cup sour cream
- 15 oz. cherry compote

DIRECTIONS:
1. Preheat oven to 375°.
2. Combine graham cracker crumbs, melted butter, and 1/4 cup sugar well. Press evenly into 9" pie pan. Bake 8-10 minutes and cool. Lower oven to 325°.
3. Blend cream cheese and remaining sugar. Add eggs one at time, blending well. Add vanilla and sour cream.
4. Pour into crust and bake for 1 hour or until cake is firm when lightly shaken. Remove and let cool, then refrigerate for an hour.
5. Spoon cherry compote over the top and serve.

My personal party night food photos of "Good Bite of Good Chuck" and "Munch It":

2007

The 79th Academy Awards® **Host: Ellen DeGeneres**
The Dolby Theater **February 25, 2007**

This was a fairly difficult year to create. But as usual, my trusty friends and family made great suggestions that formed the final menu.

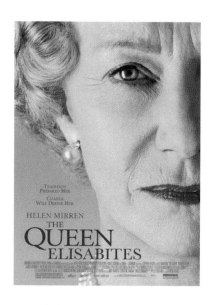

The Queen – THE QUEEN ELIZABITES

What better way to honor British royal-"tea" than with these two easy and tasty finger sandwiches!

INGREDIENTS:

- 1 loaf White bread
- 2 Cucumbers, peeled, seeded, and sliced thinly
- 8 oz. Cream cheese
- 1/4 Sour cream
- 1/2 tsp. Salt
- 1/2 tsp. fresh dill, chopped
- 1/4 lb. Ham , sliced thinly
- 1/4 lb. Swiss cheese, sliced thinly
- Dijon mustard

DIRECTIONS:

1. Cut crusts off bread slices. Set aside.
2. In a bowl, combine cream cheese, sour cream, salt, and dill. Spread on 4 slices of bread. Layer with cucumber and add another piece of bread. Cut in half.
3. Spread mustard on 4 slices of bread and layer with ham and swiss. Add another piece of bread and cut in half. Place all sandwiches on a platter and serve.

The Departed – THE PULL APARTED

I saw this excellent movie in Paris. Reading the subtitles while listening to the differing dialogue was really interesting. Viva la Paris!

INGREDIENTS:

- 1 tbsp. ground black pepper
- 4 tsp. brown sugar
- 2 tsp. cayenne pepper
- 2 tsp. chili powder
- 2 tsp. ground cumin
- 1 tbsp. paprika
- 2 tsp. + 1 pinch salt
- 2 cloves garlic, minced
- 5 lb. boneless pork shoulder
- 1/2 cup ketchup
- 2 tbsp. brown sugar
- 2 tbsp. Worcestershire sauce
- 2 tbsp. apple cider vinegar
- 1 tsp. garlic powder
- 1/4 tsp. mustard powder
- Hot sauce

DIRECTIONS:

1. Preheat oven to 400°. Lay a piece of foil on an edged baking sheet.
2. Combine black pepper, 2 tbsp. brown sugar, cayenne pepper, chili powder, cumin, paprika, 2 tsp. salt, and garlic. Place meat on foil and rub spice mix liberally all over the meat on both sides. Seal in the foil and roast for 1 hour.
3. Lower the oven to 325°, roast for 2 more hours. Remove from oven and check if the meat flakes with a fork. If not, seal and roast for an additional 30 minutes.
4. In a small saucepan on medium heat, combine ketchup, remaining brown sugar, Worcestershire sauce, vinegar, garlic powder, mustard powder, and hot sauce to taste. Stir until well blended and heated well.
5. Shred pork and combine lightly with sauce. Serve with sauce on the side.

Little Miss Sunshine – LITTLE MASH SUNSHINE

Sweet potatoes are so perfect simply roasted but when they're mashed up, they transcend their perfection!

INGREDIENTS:
- 2 lbs. sweet potatoes, peeled and cubed
- 1/2 cup butter
- 1/2 cup milk
- 3/4 cup maple syrup
- Salt & pepper

DIRECTIONS:
1. Boil potatoes in salted water until tender.
2. Drain potatoes and place in a large bowl. Add milk and mash to desired texture. Mix in butter, syrup, and salt & pepper to taste. Serve warm.

Letters From Iwo Jima – LETTUCE FROM IWO JIMA

I used the creamy ginger dressing from a local hibachi restaurant – it was the best! Using the wasabi peas gave the salad a little bite and good texture.

INGREDIENTS:
- 1 head Iceberg lettuce, washed and chopped
- Wasabi peas
- Salt & pepper
- Ginger dressing

DIRECTIONS:
1. Combine lettuce and peas in a bowl.
2. Season with salt & pepper to taste. Add dressing liberally and mix. Serve.

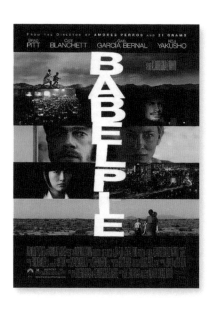

Babel – BABEL PIE

I decided to create a simple apple pie tweaked with brown sugar, which is a nod to the Mexican version.

INGREDIENTS:

- 4 granny smith apples, cored, peeled, & sliced
- 2 red delicious apples, cored, peeled, & sliced
- 1/4 cup sugar
- 3/4 cup brown sugar
- 2 tbsp. flour
- 3/4 tsp. cinnamon
- 1/4 tsp. salt
- 1/8 tsp. nutmeg
- 1 tbsp. lemon juice
- 1 package pie crusts, room temperature

DIRECTIONS:

1. Preheat oven to 425°.
2. Combine apples, sugar, brown sugar, flour, cinnamon, salt, nutmeg, and lemon juice.
3. Place one pie crust in 9" pie pan. Add apple mixture to it and cover with other pie crust. Seal edges and cut a few small slits in the top.
4. Bake for 25 minutes. Check pie – add foils to the edges if over-browning. Bake an additional 15 minutes until pie is golden brown.
5. Remove from the oven, cool, and serve.

My personal party night food photos of "The Pulled Aparted" and "Little Mash Sunshine":

2008

The 80th Academy Awards®
The Dolby Theater

Host: Jon Stewart
February 24, 2008

Jon was back for another fabulous show. This was also the first time my love, Marc Mogol, experienced my unique brand of "Oscar® madness". Needless to say, he hasn't missed a show since!

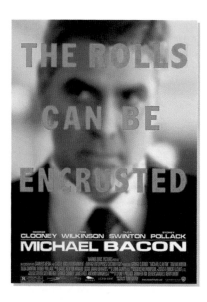

Michael Clayton: The Truth Can Be Adjusted –
MICHAEL BACON: THE ROLLS CAN BE ENCRUSTED

Yeah, a stretch, but what an old-school appetizer. When I was a kid, my mother would make these for New Year's Eve. They are surprisingly delicious!

INGREDIENTS:
- 10 pieces white bread, crusts removed
- 16 oz. whipped cream cheese.
- 2 lbs. bacon
- toothpicks

DIRECTIONS:
1. Preheat oven to 400°.
2. Spread cream cheese on each slice of bread and cut into 3 strips.
3. Place a piece of bread on a strip of bacon and roll up. Secure with toothpick.
4. Bake for 10 minutes or until bacon is done. Plate and serve.

No Country For Old Men – NO COUNTRY FOR OLD HEN

Not a funny movie at all. But in creating the poster, I cracked myself up when I added a little buddy for that scary character.

INGREDIENTS:
- 1 cup seasoned bread crumbs
- 1/4 cup grated Parmesan cheese
- 2 cups flour
- 2 large eggs, beaten
- 8 chicken cutlets, thin
- vegetable oil
- iceberg lettuce, washed and separated into leaves
- beefsteak tomatoes, sliced
- ciabatta rolls

DIRECTIONS:
1. In one dish, mix bread crumbs and cheese. Place flour on a flat dish and eggs in a bowl. Dredge cutlets in flour, then eggs (letting excess drip back into the bowl), then bread crumbs. Repeat until all are coated.
2. Pour about 1/2-1" oil in skillet and heat on high. Carefully put each cutlet in the oil. Fry until golden on both sides, about 6 minutes. Be sure that chicken is cooked thoroughly. Remove to paper-towel covered dish to absorb excess oil. Repeat until all the cutlets are fried. Serve with lettuce, tomato, and rolls to make sandwiches.

Juno – ARANJUNO

No arancini, or rice balls compare with my Nanny's, which we call "ronginis". It seemed a great choice for this selection, rice ball as Juno's belly... mozzarella filling... uh huh. Note – Nanny only used Carolina white rice. We do what she did.

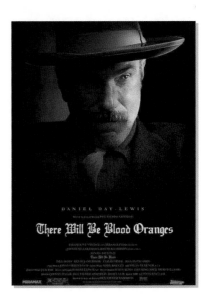

INGREDIENTS:
- salt & pepper
- 1 cup Carolina white rice
- 1/2 stick butter
- 2 large eggs, beaten
- 2-3 tbsp. grated Romano or Parmesan cheese
- 3-4 oz. packaged mozzarella
- 2 cups plain bread crumbs
- vegetable oil

DIRECTIONS:
1. Make one cup of white rice according to package directions. The water should be fully absorbed by the rice – if any remains, drain.
2. Add 1/2 stick of butter, cheese, and pepper to taste. Blend together. Let it sit until room temperature, then fold 2 eggs into rice and mix well. Set aside.
3. Chop mozzarella into small pieces. Set aside.
4. Create an "assembly line": rice, dish of bread crumbs, and mozzarella with a dish for the finished rice balls. You'll be creating about 2" rice balls.
5. Sprinkle one hand with bread crumbs, then spread rice in your palm. Sprinkle more bread crumbs over the rice, then a couple bits of mozzarella – close to create a ball. Roll in bread crumbs and place to the side. Keep going until you're out of rice. Heat a deep pot about halfway filled with oil. Then, using a small basket or slotted spoon, gingerly place rice balls in, leaving enough room to scoop them out. Lift out when they become a golden brown. Place on paper towel to absorb excess oil. Keep going until they're all cooked and mangia!

There Will Be Blood – THERE WILL BE BLOOD ORANGES

Blood oranges are only available at certain times of the year. It was extremely fortuitous to have them for this juicy salad!

INGREDIENTS:
- 1 bulb endive, washed
- 1 head radicchio, washed
- 1 head romaine, washed
- 3 blood oranges
- 1/4 cup extra virgin olive oil
- 2 tbsp. apple cider vinegar
- salt & pepper

DIRECTIONS:
1. Rip endive, radicchio, and romaine into bite-sized pieces and put in a large bowl. Peel and cut up 2 oranges and add to salad.
2. Halve and squeeze remaining orange into a small container.
3. Add olive oil, vinegar, salt & pepper to taste. Stir and mix into the salad. Serve.

Atonement – ACONEMENT

The simple ice cream cone is one of life's most enjoyable treats. Using it as a dish was fabulous. I chose four ice cream flavors that night. Choose as many or few as you like.

INGREDIENTS:
- chocolate sprinkles
- rainbow sprinkles
- hot fudge
- ice cream
- 1 package sugar cones

DIRECTIONS:
1. Place sprinkles in small bowls with serving spoons. Warm the hot fudge.
2. Assemble by placing 2 scoops ice cream in a dish, add sprinkles and/or hot fudge to taste, and top with a cone "hat" or just crumble it over the ice cream.

My personal party night food photos of "Michael Bacon: The Rolls Can Be Encrusted" and "No Country for Old Hen":

2009

The 81st Academy Awards®   **Host: Hugh Jackman**
The Dolby Theater   **February 22, 2009**

Now this was a dreamy year! Song and dance and actor and all-around entertainer man, Hugh Jackman, graced the stage with his overall razzmatazz! So easy on the eyes... so wonderful as host.

Slumdog Millionaire – HOT DOG EXTRAORDINAIRE

Like the character in the movie, I took the ordinary and made it extraordinary. I repeated the mini hot dogs but put them with four dipping sauces.

INGREDIENTS:
- 1 100-ct package mini cocktail franks in puff pastry, frozen
- dijon mustard
- yellow mustard
- satay peanut sauce
- red curry sauce

DIRECTIONS:
1. Prepare mini cocktail franks according to package directions.
2. Spoon each condiment into separate bowls.
3. Serve on a large platter and dip away.

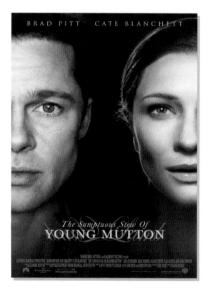

The Curious Case of Benjamin Button – THE SCRUMPTIOUS STEW OF YOUNG MUTTON

What to make was somewhat curious. I made the case that if mutton is "old" lamb and the movie focuses on a strange aging phenomenon, best to "stew" on it.

INGREDIENTS:
- extra virgin olive oil
- 2 lbs. lamb, cubed
- 3 carrots, peeled and chopped
- 3 large potatoes, peeled and chopped
- 1 large yellow onion, quartered and sliced
- 8 oz. plain tomato sauce
- 1 cup beef bouillon/stock/broth
- 1 cup red wine
- 1 tbsp. fresh rosemary
- salt & pepper

DIRECTIONS:
1. In a stockpot on medium heat, drizzle olive oil and brown/sear the meat.
2. Add onions and cook for 3 minutes.
3. Add carrots, potatoes, tomato sauce, beef stock, wine, rosemary, and salt & pepper to taste. Bring up to a boil then set to simmer and cover.
4. After about 30 minutes, taste to see if it needs any additional seasoning. Add if necessary.
5. Continue to simmer another 30-45 minutes. When the meat is tender and the liquid thickened, it's ready to serve!

The Reader – THE KNEADER

This movie takes place in Germany and deals with a crusty "twist" so serving marble rye bread, which is rye and pumpernickel breads intertwined, was the perfect accompaniment to the lamb stew.

INGREDIENTS:
- A great bread department at the market or bread bakery

DIRECTIONS:
1. Purchase bread.
2. Cut into large hunks and serve!

Frost/Nixon – NIX-ON/FROST

OK, go with me on this one. This interview was a big deal at the time. The movie captured it quite well. Nixon was a seemingly cold dude. I put a "nix on" that "frost" and created a salad with a warm bacon dressing. Get it? Get it???

INGREDIENTS:
- 1 head green leaf lettuce, washed
- 16 oz. baby spinach, rinsed
- 1 small vidalia (sweet) onion, chopped
- 6 strips bacon
- 2 shallots, minced
- 1/2 cup red wine vinegar
- 1/4 tsp. salt
- 1/2 tsp. pepper

DIRECTIONS:
1. Rip lettuce to bite-sized pieces and put in a large bowl with spinach and onion. Set aside.
2. Cook bacon in a skillet until well done. Add shallots and cook until translucent. Whisk in vinegar, salt, and pepper.
3. Pour over salad, mix and serve immediately.

Milk – MILK TOAST

Someone who is a "milk toast" is not a strong person. Harvey Milk was the exact opposite. There was nothing "plain" or "vanilla" about him. And so, with tongue in cheek, I chose cinnamon pastry sticks and vanilla ice cream.

INGREDIENTS:

- 1 package puffed pastry dough, room temperature
- 1/2 cup sugar
- 2 tsp. cinnamon
- 2 large eggs, beaten
- vanilla ice cream

DIRECTIONS:

1. Preheat oven to 350°. Place parchment paper on baking sheet.
2. Combine sugar and cinnamon in a small bowl. Set aside.
3. Roll out dough and brush with eggs. Liberally sprinkle cinnamon-sugar blend over the pastry.
4. Cut dough diagonally into 1" strips, then cut in half length-wise.
5. Gently twist each piece and place on baking sheets 1" apart.
6. Bake about 10-12 minutes or until golden. Cool on baking sheet for 5 minutes to set before moving to cooling racks.
7. Place a scoop of ice cream in a bowl adding 1-2 "toasts" and serve.

My personal party night food photos of "Hot Dog Extraordinaire" and "Milk Toast":

2010

The 82nd Academy Awards®   Hosts: Alec Baldwin
The Dolby Theater   March 2, 2010   Steve Martin

A memorable year. Ten films were nominated for Best Picture - double the dishes! AND, we missed the much anticipated opener due to a cable company contract dispute. The channel suddenly started to broadcast 15 minutes in, but I changed cable service as soon as I could. We did have a lot more tasty dishes though!

An Education – AN EGGUQUICHEION

This quiche comes from wonderful Joe Becwar, who has been featured prominently in the world of KitchAnnette. We have been cooking together for years, creating lots of fun and flavorful fare.

INGREDIENTS:
- 3 large eggs
- 1 cup milk
- salt & pepper
- 10 oz. spinach, chopped frozen, thawed and drained
- 2 plum tomatoes diced & drained
- 1 small yellow onion, chopped
- 6 oz. feta cheese, crumbled
- 1 deep dish pie crust, frozen

DIRECTIONS:
1. Preheat oven to 375°.
2. In large bowl, whisk eggs, milk, salt & pepper to taste. Mix in spinach, tomatoes, onion, and feta.
3. Place frozen pie crust on a baking sheet and pour mixture into the crust. Bake at for 45-55 minutes or until firm to touch. Let cool and serve.

District 9 – DESHRIMP 9

It would seem like a far reach but there are characters called "prawns" in the movie. That cracked me up and made the choice very clear.

INGREDIENTS:
- 1 lb. jumbo shrimp, cleaned and cooked (frozen)
- 16 oz. cocktail sauce
- 1 lemon, cut into wedges

DIRECTIONS:
1. Thaw shrimp according to package directions.
2. Pour the cocktail sauce into a serving bowl and surround with shrimp, and lemon wedges.

The Blind Side – THE BLIND SLIDERS

Football, little hamburgers, touchdown!

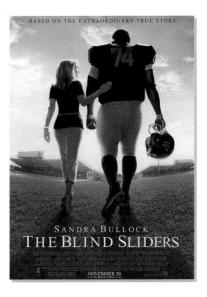

INGREDIENTS:
- 2 lbs. ground chuck
- 1 package dried onion soup mix
- package of small rolls

DIRECTIONS:
1. In a large bowl, mix meat with onion soup mix. Shape into about 16 patties.
2. Heat a large grill pan and grill patties about 3 minutes on each side or until cooked to desired doneness.
3. Serve with rolls!

A Serious Man – A BI-CURIOUS HAM

I had a lot of fun with the poster and created a taste-provoking version of a sweet & savory ham thanks to the wonderful Barbara Morgan DeBisschop.

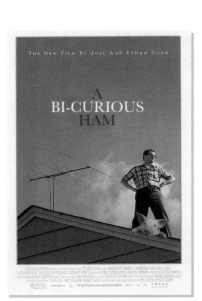

INGREDIENTS:
- 1 spiral ham
- extra virgin olive oil
- 1 red bell pepper, chopped
- 1 green bell pepper, chopped
- salt & pepper
- 15 oz. pineapple chunks in natural juices

DIRECTIONS:
1. Cook ham according to package instructions.
2. In a skillet, add a drizzle or two of olive oil and sauté the peppers until tender, seasoning with salt & pepper to taste.
3. Add pineapple chunks with juice, mix, and cover. Simmer for about 15 minutes.
4. When ham is ready, place on a platter and smother it in the pineapple & pepper sauce. It's ready to serve.

Inglorious Bastards – CALIFLOURIOUS BREADSTERDS

Oh, this was a stretch but I made it work with the poster. Ha! And it's really good.

INGREDIENTS:
- 1 head cauliflower, cleaned & cut into small pieces
- extra virgin olive oil
- salt & pepper
- 1/2 cup seasoned bread crumbs
- 2 tbsp. butter, melted

DIRECTIONS:
1. Preheat oven to 350°.
2. Parboil cauliflower, drain, and put in casserole dish.
3. Toss with a drizzle of olive oil and salt & pepper to taste.
4. Bake for 25-30 minutes and check for tenderness.
5. In a small bowl, mix bread crumbs and butter. Spread evenly over cauliflower. And bake an additional 3 minutes or until crumbs brown. Serve while hot.

The Hurt Locker — THE HURT LATKE

Unfortunately, there was a snafu that day so my mom brought knishes as you'll see in my photos. Here is the recipe I had planned to make, and have made many times since. Using the cayenne and green peppers makes the flavor explode!

INGREDIENTS:
- 2 lbs. potatoes, peeled
- 1 small yellow onion
- 1/4 cup green bell pepper, diced
- 2 large eggs, beaten
- 2 tbsp. matzo meal
- 1/4 tsp. cayenne pepper
- salt & pepper
- vegetable oil

DIRECTIONS:
1. Grate or shred potatoes. Place in a large bowl. Grate or shred onion and place in the same bowl. Add pepper, eggs and matzo meal, cayenne, and salt & pepper to taste.
2. Pour oil in a skillet. Heat on medium until oil is hot. Using a tablespoon, drop potato mixture carefully into the oil. Fry and turn over until golden brown – about 3 minutes. Place on paper towels to drain excess oil. Repeat until mixture has all been fried. Serve while hot.

Precious: Based on the novel Push by Sapphire –
PROSCIUCIOUS: BASED ON THE DISH "PEAS WITH ONIONS"

Yes, a STRETCH!!! I have no defense except – it was gooo-ooood!

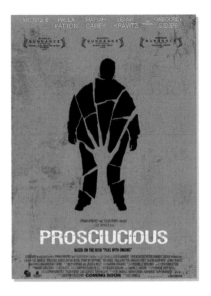

INGREDIENTS:
- extra virgin olive oil
- 1 small yellow onion, diced
- salt & pepper
- 3 strips prosciutto, diced
- 15 oz. peas, room temperature

DIRECTIONS:
1. In a skillet on medium heat, add 2 drizzles of olive oil and onion. Season well with salt & pepper. Cook until onions are translucent.
2. Add prosciutto and cook for 3 minutes before adding the peas.
3. When peas are well coated and tender, remove from heat and serve.

Up – TOSS UP

I loved this movie more than I thought I could. It was so well done. I knew it should be honored with a traditional tossed salad!

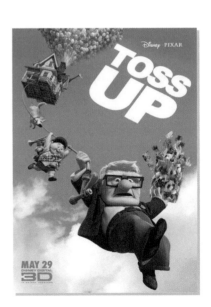

INGREDIENTS:
- 1 head romaine, washed
- 3 beefsteak or stem tomatoes
- 1 small red onion, chopped
- 1 hothouse cucumber, halved and sliced
- vegetable oil
- white balsamic vinegar
- salt & pepper

DIRECTIONS:
1. Rip up romaine and cut tomatoes into bite-sized pieces and place in large bowl. Mix in onion and cucumber.
2. Drizzle in a generous amount of oil and about half that of vinegar. Season with salt & pepper. Toss well and serve.

Avatar – AVATART

This was a "no brainer" for me – blue people equals blueberries – blueberry tart!

INGREDIENTS:
- 1 cup + 2 tbsp. flour
- 1 pinch salt
- 2/3 cup + 2 tbsp. sugar
- 1/2 cup butter
- 1 tbsp. white vinegar
- 5 cups blueberries, washed and dried
- 1/2 tsp. cinnamon

DIRECTIONS:
1. Preheat oven to 400°. Mix 1 cup flour, salt, and 2 tbsp. sugar. Add butter to create course crumbs. Add vinegar and form into dough.
2. Using a tart pan, press dough evenly across bottom and up sides.
3. In a large bowl, toss 3 cups blueberries, remaining sugar and flour with cinnamon and pour into dough.
4. Bake for 50 minutes or until filling is bubbling and crust is browned. Remove to cooling rack.
5. Pour in remaining blueberries and let cool. Remove pan's rim and serve!

Up In The Air – UPSIDE DOWN PEAR

I cracked up when I created the poster... that little pear hangin' out in the airport. In the movie, George & Anna's characters were an upside down pear errrr... pair.

INGREDIENTS:
- 1/2 cup + 3 tbsp. butter
- 3/4 cup brown sugar
- 4 pears, sliced thickly
- maraschino cherries, stemmed
- 1 cup sugar
- 2 large eggs
- 1 tsp. vanilla
- 1/2 cup milk
- 1-1/2 cup flour
- 2 tsp. baking powder
- 1/2 tsp. salt

DIRECTIONS:
1. Preheat oven to 350°. On low heat, in a 9" baking pan, melt 3 tbsp. butter with brown sugar. Turn off the heat and arrange pears, slightly overlapping, in the pan. Add cherries to the center to fully fill the surface.
2. In a bowl, mix flour, salt and baking powder. In a separate bowl, mix remaining butter, sugar, eggs, and vanilla. Slowly add flour mixture and milk.
3. Pour batter into the pan, spread evenly over the pears. Put pan on a baking sheet and bake for 50 minutes until brown and testing toothpick comes out clean. The center should spring back to the touch. Place cake on cooling rack.
4. After 5 minutes, run a butter knife around the edge of cake, place a dish over it, and slowly turn the cake over – use mitts! Lift the pan off and let cool fully (if any fruit stuck to the pan, scrap off and put back in place on the cake). Serve!

My personal party night food photos:

2011

The 83rd Academy Awards®   **Hosts: Anne Hathaway**
The Dolby Theater   February 27, 2011   James Franco

This was quite a show. The buzz was it was going to be bad. I really did my best to support them and watch with an open mind, but… it was not good. Luckily the food was exceptional!

The Kids Are All Right – THE PIGS ARE ROLLED TIGHT

An often reprised dish, piggies in blankets are perfect bites that put a smile on everyone's face. This time I didn't go the frozen route! Always better!

INGREDIENTS:
- 2 lb. mini hot dogs or 30 regular hot dogs, halved
- 1 package puffed pastry, room temperature
- whole grain mustard

DIRECTIONS:
1. Preheat oven to 450°.
2. Roll out each sheet of dough to 14" x 12" length. Cut into strips 1" x 3.5" and roll hot dogs up "tight".
3. Place on baking sheet and bake about 20 minutes or until pastry is golden brown. Plate and serve with mustard!

Black Swan – BLACK PRAWN

This was really "pretty" easy to create. Less blackened, more spicy!

INGREDIENTS:
- 3 tbsp. extra virgin olive oil
- 3 cloves of garlic, minced
- 1 lb. large shrimp, cleaned
- 1/4 tsp. cayenne pepper
- 1/4 tsp. ancho chili pepper
- salt & pepper
- 1 lemon

DIRECTIONS:
1. In a skillet, over medium heat, add olive oil and garlic. As garlic browns, add in the shrimp with cayenne and ancho chili peppers, salt & pepper to taste.
2. Cook about 2 minutes on each side and remove from heat. Plate and serve!

Inception – INDIPTION

If you've seen the film, it focuses on entering dreams and going through layers. I chose to go through 5 layers of dip with chips to commemorate it!

INGREDIENTS:
- 15 oz. refried beans
- 1-1/2 cups guacamole
- 1-1/2 cups sour cream
- 5 plum tomatoes, diced
- 8 oz. cheddar cheese, shredded
- 8 oz. monterey jack cheese, shredded
- tortilla chips

DIRECTIONS:
1. In a deep dish, assemble ingredients – refried beans, guacamole, sour cream, and tomatoes.
2. In a separate bowl, mix the cheddar and Monterey jack cheese together. Add to the dish to complete. Enjoy with chips!

The Social Network – THE SO-CALLED NOT PORK

This was not only a stretch but also a tough poster to create. Have you "liked" the KitchAnnette page on Facebook yet? Haaa!

INGREDIENTS:
- 2 lb. flank steak
- coarse sea salt
- freshly ground black pepper

DIRECTIONS:
1. Mix generous amounts of salt and pepper together and rub on both sides of the meat. Move meat to broiler pan.
2. Place meat in broiler on the lower rung, leaving the door slightly ajar, and cook 4-5 minutes on each side for medium doneness.
3. Remove from heat. Place on carving board and cut in thin slices on the bias against the grain. Pour juice from pan over the top and serve.

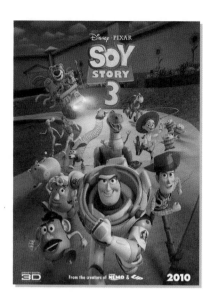

Toy Story 3 – SOY STORY 3

The funniest thing is that the definition of "edamame" states they are "immature" soy beans. How perfect for this!

INGREDIENTS:
- 2 tbsp. vegetable oil
- 3 cloves garlic, chopped
- 1 head broccoli, cut to florets
- 1 lb. edamame, cooked and shelled
- 8 oz. water chestnuts
- 3/4 cup teriyaki sauce
- fresh ground black pepper

DIRECTIONS:
1. In a sauté pan over medium heat, add oil and garlic until it begins to brown.
2. Add broccoli, cooking for about 10 minutes. Add edamame and water chestnuts with teriyaki sauce and pepper to taste. When heated through, remove from heat, plate, and serve!

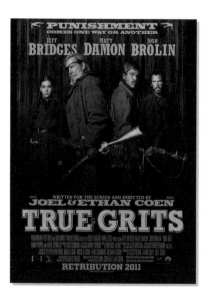

True Grit – TRUE GRITS

Really… I didn't even BLINK for this one. It told me what it was going to be.

INGREDIENTS:
- 3/4 cup grits, quick-style
- 4 oz. cheddar cheese
- 3 cups water
- salt & pepper

DIRECTIONS:
1. Boil water in a saucepan. Add grits and salt. Simmer and stir for about 5 minutes until it starts to thicken.
2. Add the cheese and pepper to taste, stirring thoroughly.
3. Remove from heat and serve.

The Fighter – THE BITER

The crumbly crunch of a crouton with the fresh bite of lettuce always packs a one-two punch.

INGREDIENTS:
- 1 head radicchio, washed
- 1 head romaine, washed
- 3-4 cloves garlic, minced
- 8 oz. croutons
- extra virgin olive oil
- white balsamic vinegar
- salt & pepper

DIRECTIONS:
1. Chop radicchio and romaine. Place in a large bowl. Add garlic and croutons and mix well.
2. Drizzle a generous amount of olive oil and vinegar to taste. Season with salt & pepper. Take a big BITE!

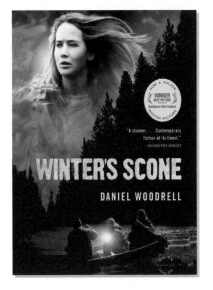

Winter's Bone – WINTER'S SCONE

There's nothing like a warm delicious scone on a cold winter's day – or any day!

INGREDIENTS:
- 3 cups flour
- 1/2 cup sugar
- 2 tsp. baking powder
- 1/4 tsp. baking soda
- 1/2 tsp. salt
- 4 oz. butter, cold and cut into small pieces
- 1/2 cup milk
- 1/2 cup plain yogurt or sour cream
- 3/4 cup dried cranberries

DIRECTIONS:
1. Preheat oven to 375°. Mix flour, sugar, baking powder, baking soda, and salt until well combined.
2. Add butter. Mix until it's a crumbly consistency. Add yogurt and mix. Slowly add in milk. Mix until dough forms.
3. Divide dough in half and cover with plastic wrap. Refrigerate overnight. Place dough on floured surface. Shape into 12" log. Roll until it is 12" x 5". Press half the cranberries into the dough. Fold dough in half length-wise. Cut into triangles to baking sheet lined with parchment. Repeat with other dough. Sprinkle with sugar.
4. Bake for 18-20 minutes until slightly browned. Cool and serve.

127 Hours – 127 SOURS

Hearing something is "sour" is rarely appetizing but the lemon icing on these anginette cookies is really sweet. And YES, I served exactly 127 of them!

INGREDIENTS:
- 3/4 stick butter
- 1/2 cup sugar
- 1 tsp. vanilla
- 3 large eggs
- 2-2.5 cups flour
- 1 pinch salt
- 6 tsp. baking powder
- 2 cups confectioners sugar
- 2 tbsp. milk
- 1 tsp. lemon juice

DIRECTIONS:
1. Cream together the butter, sugar, vanilla. Add eggs, flour, salt, baking powder and mix. The dough will be "thick".
2. Spoon 1/2 teaspoon-size of dough per cookie onto a baking sheet. Bake in a 350° oven for 10-12 minutes. Place on cooling rack.
3. Mix confectioner's sugar, milk, and lemon juice in a bowl. Taste to see if it's tart or sweet enough for you and adjust.
4. Holding the bottom edge of the cookie, generously dip it top-first into the bowl then place on wax paper to dry.

The King's Speech – THE KING'S PEACH

The idea for this one was so intuitive. And this cobbler was so good, it left everyone speechless (or s-peach-less)!

INGREDIENTS:
- 1 package puffed pastry
- 1 large can sliced peaches
- apricot preserves

DIRECTIONS:
1. Preheat oven to 350°.
2. Roll each sheet of dough onto an edged cookie pan, form dough up the edges to create tart shell.
3. Lay peach slices evenly over the dough. Brushed apricot jam on peaches and edges of dough.
4. Bake for 15 minutes or until edges brown.

My personal party night food photos:

2012

The 84th Academy Awards®   **Host: Billy Crystal**
The Dolby Theater   **February 26, 2012**

This was the first year that the menu really became cohesive, having a general "French bistro" flavor and feel. If you remove the movies, you could serve this menu as is. I love that! It's the new challenge I've incorporated into creating the menus.

War Horse – WARM BORSCHT

This "warm" movie about Joey takes place around World War I. With Russia as an ally in that war, this soup couldn't be "beet".

INGREDIENTS:
- 2 quarts beef bouillon, broth, or stock
- 5 fresh beets, peeled and diced
- 1 large potato, peeled and diced
- 1/2 head red cabbage, chopped
- 2 tbsp. apple cider vinegar
- salt & pepper
- 16 oz. sour cream or Greek yogurt
- fresh or dried dill
- crusty pumpernickel bread

DIRECTIONS:
1. In a large stockpot over high heat, add beef stock, beets, potato, cabbage, vinegar, and salt & pepper to taste. Once it's boiling, lower the heat to simmer.
2. Check it after about 45 minutes. The veggies should be soft. To make it smooth, either use an immersion or regular blender.
3. Serve with dollop of sour cream or Greek yogurt, garnishing with a touch of dill! Enjoy with crusty pumpernickel bread

The Tree of Life – THE BRIE OF LIFE

Everyone always enjoys a hunk of warm, gooey sweet/savory cheese!

INGREDIENTS:
- A round or wedge(s) of brie cheese
- apricot jam
- sliced almonds
- black pepper
- crackers or bread

DIRECTIONS:
1. Preheat oven to 300°.
2. Place brie in the center of a cookie sheet. Liberally spread apricot jam over it. Sprinkle with a layer of sliced almonds and add fresh ground black pepper to taste.
3. Bake for about 15 minutes or until the Brie is soft and gooey. Serve on a plate with a variety of crackers and crusty bread!

Extremely Loud & Incredibly Close – EXTREMELY PROUD – INCREDIBLE ROAST

I'm a New Yorker so this movie was very relevant. It was a time of people uniting and comforting one another – roasted chicken is a universal comfort food.

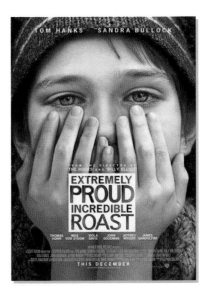

INGREDIENTS:
- 1 whole chicken
- extra virgin olive oil
- 1 orange, quartered
- 1 apple, quartered
- 1 lemon, quartered
- fresh herbs – rosemary, thyme, sage
- salt & pepper

DIRECTIONS:
1. Preheat oven at 450°.
2. Unwrap and wash chicken. Make sure to keep washing your hands – raw chicken must be worked with carefully. Dispose of the "innards". Rub the chicken with olive oil, top and bottom. Liberally sprinkle with salt & pepper.
3. Fill the cavity with orange, lemon, and apple. Add fresh herbs inside and out.
4. Place chicken in a roasting pan and bake for 10-15 minutes until top is browned. Lower the oven to 350°, remove chicken from the oven and turn it over. Season with salt & pepper, and put it in the oven for 35-40 minutes, or until the inside temperature of the chicken is no less than 155°. Remove from the oven but leave the thermometer in – the chicken will continue to cook out of the oven. When it reaches 165°, it's ready to plate and serve.

The Help – THE HELPING OF MASHED POTATOES

There's nothing like a healthy helping of mashed potatoes!

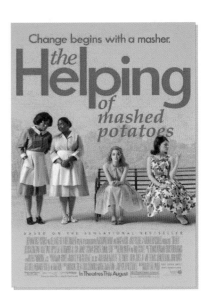

INGREDIENTS:
- 2 lbs. Idaho potatoes, peeled
- 1/2 stick butter
- 1/2 cup milk (more if needed)
- salt & pepper

DIRECTIONS:
1. Boil potatoes in salted water until tender.
2. Drain potatoes. In a large bowl, add potatoes, butter, and milk. Mash until they are almost smooth. Add salt and pepper to taste.

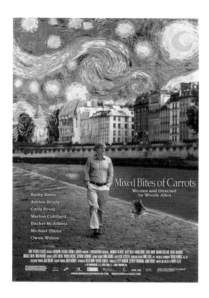

For Midnight in Paris – MIXED BITES OF CARROTS

After New York, Paris is my favorite city. Adding a time travel nuance in this movie made it even more alluring.

INGREDIENTS:
- 1 lb. orange carrots, peeled and chopped into chunks
- 1 lb. purple (or any other colored) carrots, peeled and chopped into chunks
- 2 medium yellow onions, chopped
- salt & pepper
- 1/4 cup vegetable oil

DIRECTIONS:
1. Preheat oven to 350°. In a large pot, parboil – boil for a minute or two – the carrots. Empty all the water but about 1/4 cup.
2. Add in the onions & salt & pepper to taste, and about 1/4 cup vegetable oil. Mix well until carrots and onions are well coated.
3. Pour into a roasting pan and place in the oven for about 20-25 minutes – check to make sure they don't burn. And there you have it! Plate & serve.

For Hugo – HUGOAT CHEESE SALAD

This movie was so amazing, again taking place in Paris and becoming an homage to the work of Georges Méliès. I just had to "build" a magical salad!

INGREDIENTS:
- 1 head romaine lettuce
- 1 head radicchio
- 1 head endive
- 1/4 cup dried cranberries
- 1/4 cup walnuts, chopped
- 6 oz. chevre/goat cheese
- salt & pepper
- 1/4 cup extra virgin olive oil
- 2 tbsp. seedless raspberry jam
- 1/4 cup apple cider vinegar

DIRECTIONS:
1. Wash and break up romaine lettuce, radicchio, and endive into a large bowl.
2. Add dried cranberries and walnuts, season with salt & pepper to taste.
3. To make the raspberry vinaigrette, combine oil, jam, vinegar, and salt & pepper to taste. Pour over the salad and mix well.
4. Finish with crumbling a GENEROUS amount of goat cheese into the salad. Delicately fold in and serve!

The Artist – THE TARTIST

This is more of an apple torte than tart. It will leave you as speechless as the film!

INGREDIENTS:
- 1/2 cup + 3 tbsp. butter
- 1 cup sugar divided
- 3/4 tsp. vanilla, divided
- 1 cup flour
- 8 oz. cream cheese
- 1 large egg
- 1 tsp. cinnamon
- 3 granny smith apples, sliced
- 1 red delicious apple, sliced
- 3 tbsp. apricot jam
- 1/4 cup sliced almonds

DIRECTIONS:
1. Preheat oven to 450°. For the crust, mix 1/2 cup butter, 1/3 cup sugar, and 1/4 tsp. vanilla. Blend in flour. Spread evenly onto bottom and sides of a 9" spring form pan.
2. In a bowl, combine cream cheese with 1/4 cup sugar. Add egg and 1/2 tsp. vanilla. Pour into the pan.
3. In a different bowl, combine 1/3 cup sugar and cinnamon. Toss with apples. Arrange slices over the cream cheese layer. Sprinkle evenly with almonds.
4. Bake for 10 minutes. Reduce heat to 400°. Bake for 25 minutes and remove from the oven for a moment.
5. In small sauce pan, melt 3 tbsp. butter and add apricot jam. Stir to create glaze and drizzle over the torte. Place it back in the oven for no more than 1 minute. Set on a cooling rack and leave in pan until cool. Remove pan. Serve!

The Descendants – THE DECADENCE

OK... this is one of the famous "stretches" but adding the macadamia nuts was the connector! Aloha!

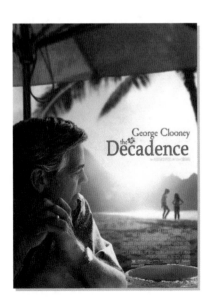

INGREDIENTS:
- 1/2 cup flour
- 1/4 tsp. salt
- 2 squares (2 oz.) unsweetened chocolate
- 1/2 cup butter
- 2 large eggs
- 1 cup sugar
- 1 tsp. vanilla
- 1/2 cup macadamia nuts

DIRECTIONS:
1. Preheat oven to 350°. In a large bowl, sift flour and salt.
2. Melt chocolate and butter over low heat. Set aside to cool.
3. In separate bowl, beat eggs until foamy. Add sugar. Continue beating until well blended. Stir in cooled chocolate and vanilla. Add flour and mix thoroughly.
4. Pour batter into greased 9" pan. Even out top & sprinkle with macadamia nuts.
5. Bake for 10-12 minutes or until tester comes out clean. Remove from oven, let cool in pan for 10 minutes, then remove to cooling rack. Enjoy!

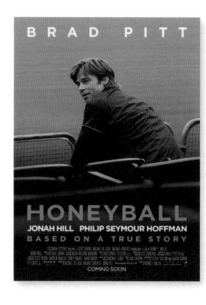

Moneyball – HONEYBALL

Mine came out a bit less round that night but the flavor definitely hit a home run!

INGREDIENTS:
- 1 cup water
- 1/2 cup butter
- 1 cup flour
- pinch of salt
- 4 large eggs
- 1/2 cup honey
- 1/4 cup sugar
- 1/4 tsp. cinnamon
- confectioners sugar

DIRECTIONS:
1. Preheat oven to 350°.
2. Put water and butter in a large pot and bring to a full boil. Stir in flour and salt until it becomes a big ball.
3. Put dough ball in a large mixing bowl. Beat the eggs in well – one at a time.
4. Using a teaspoon, spoon dough and make into balls – place on a cookie sheet. Bake 15-20 minutes or until golden brown and cool.
5. In a saucepan, bring honey, sugar, and cinnamon to a boil, stirring, to make the glaze.
6. In a bowl, coat the dough balls with the glaze. Add a sprinkle of confectioners sugar. Arrange on a platter and serve.

My personal party night food photos:

2013

The 85th Academy Awards® Host: Seth MacFarlane
The Dolby Theater   February 24, 2013

Having Seth MacFarlane host was a stroke of genius.
I am a fan of his humor and thought he nailed it. The
reviews were split. I hope he is invited back! Oh... the
food... it was incredible! Every dish is rich and
flavorful. Every dish is a snap to make, too.

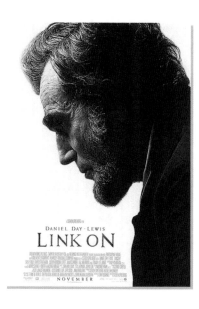

Lincoln – LINK ON

Being born on his birthday, I am forever "linked" to him.

INGREDIENTS:
- 2 lbs. skinny sausage cut to 2-3" pieces
- polenta log, sliced into 1/2" rounds for each sausage piece
- 1 28 oz. can crushed tomatoes
- 1 medium yellow onion, diced
- extra virgin olive oil
- salt & pepper

DIRECTIONS:
1. Preheat oven to 450°. Place polenta rounds on baking sheet. Brush olive oil on each, add salt & pepper to taste. Bake for 10-15 minutes until slightly brown.
2. Drizzle olive oil in a saucepan, heat and sauté onion over medium heat for about 5 minutes until they become translucent. Add the tomatoes, salt & pepper to taste, and a touch more of olive oil. Stir and let simmer.
3. In a frying pan, add 1/2" olive oil and on high heat, add the cut sausage pieces. Brown thoroughly, which should take about 8-10 minutes.
4. Plate the rounds, add a piece of sausage to the top of each, and spoon a bit of tomato sauce over the top. Voila!

Silver Lining Playbook – SILVER LINING CRABCAKES

The idea to have mini crab cakes in silver mini muffin cups came from the movie – they made "crabby snacks and homemades" for the game.

INGREDIENTS:
- 1/4 cup red bell pepper, finely diced
- 1/4 cup yellow bell pepper, finely diced
- 4 scallions, diced
- 2 tbsp. fresh parsley, minced
- 8 oz. lump crabmeat
- 1 large egg
- 2 cups plain bread crumbs
- 1/2 tsp. cayenne pepper
- salt & pepper
- extra virgin olive oil spray

DIRECTIONS:
1. Preheat oven to 375°. Prepare mini muffin tin with silver mini muffin liners.
2. Mix peppers, scallions, parsley, crabmeat, egg, 1-2 heaping tsp. bread crumbs, cayenne pepper, salt & pepper to taste.
3. Pour remaining breadcrumbs in a bowl. Take a spoonful of crab cake mixture, form a ball, coat with bread crumbs, and sprtiz olive on each before placing in muffin liners.
4. Bake for about 15 minutes until golden. Note: If you'd rather fry them in oil on the stove, do not add the olive oil – instead coat the pan and fry each before placing in silver muffin liners. These will SCORE!

Zero Dark Thirty – ZERO DARK TURKEY

It was a tough one to get to, but it worked perfectly to have a zero, or no dark meat turkey dish using an exotic mix of spices.

INGREDIENTS:
- 1 5 lb. turkey breast
- 2 cups plain yogurt
- 1 yellow onion, chopped
- 3-4 cloves garlic
- 6-8 slivers fresh ginger
- 2 tsp. curry
- 1 tsp. cumin
- 1 tsp. dried cilantro
- 1/2 tsp. cinnamon
- 1/4 cup lemon juice
- 1/2 tsp cayenne pepper
- salt & pepper

DIRECTIONS:
1. Preheat oven to 450°. In food processor or blender, add all ingredients except salt & pepper and the turkey (ha) and pulse until it's a thick and creamy consistency. Refrigerate for at least an hour.
2. Place the turkey breast in a roasting pan, adding salt & pepper to taste before coating with half the yogurt mixture. Reserve half the yogurt mixture to serve later.
3. Place turkey in the oven for about 1 hour or until the internal temperature at its thickest spot reaches 165°. Check after 30 minutes - if the top is already brown, place foil over the top.
4. Once it's out of the oven, let it rest a few minutes, carve, and plate with the reserve of yogurt mixture!

Les Miserables – LES MISERABES

I dreamed a dream of greens done riiiiiight... One bite mooooore... Love-ly vegg-ies cooking in the pan... If you know the songs, you'll appreciate those parody phrases!

INGREDIENTS:
- 1 bunch broccoli rabe, cleaned and stems cut
- 3-4 shallots, finely sliced
- 1 lemon's zest
- 1 stick butter
- salt & pepper

DIRECTIONS:
1. In a large sauté pan on medium heat, melt butter and cook shallots until translucent.
2. Add lemon zest, salt & pepper to taste, and broccoli rabe – mix and cover. The broccoli rabe will shrink down a bit.
3. In 7-8 minutes, it should be done but try a piece first. Some prefer it a little crunchier whereas others like it softer.
4. Take this from pan to plate and enjoy hot!

Django Unchained – DMANGO ENGRAINED

I knew I had to use mango but thanks to my friend Eileen Congdon's suggestion of using quinoa, it all came together so deliciously!

INGREDIENTS:
- 1 cup quinoa
- extra virgin olive oil
- 1 jalapeño pepper, diced
- 1 mango, cubed
- 3-4 cloves garlic, minced
- 1/2 cup fresh cilantro, chopped
- 1/4 cup fresh parsley, chopped
- 1/2 cup raisins
- 1 small tomato, chopped
- juice of 1 lime'
- salt & pepper

DIRECTIONS:
1. Prepare quinoa according to package instructions. Set aside.
2. Drizzle olive oil in a sauté pan. Add jalapeño, mango, garlic and sauté over medium heat until garlic starts to brown and mango soften.
3. Add in remaining ingredients, mixing while it cook, for 5-10 minutes until all heated through. Plate and serve.

Beast of the Southern Wild – BEETS OF THE SOUTHERN SALAD

A fresh, salad using peppery baby arugula and rich beets with feta cheese and a light citrus vinaigrette is almost a meal in itself!

INGREDIENTS:
- 1 16 oz. can whole red and/or golden beets, chopped
- 1/2 small red onion, halved and sliced
- 16 oz. baby arugula
- salt & pepper
- 1/4 cup lemon juice
- 1/4 orange juice
- extra virgin olive oil
- 3-4 oz. crumbled feta cheese

DIRECTIONS:
1. In a large bowl, mix beets, red onion, baby arugula, salt & pepper to taste.
2. In a smaller container, add the juices, a little less than 1/4 cup olive oil, salt & pepper to taste.
3. Right before serving, add the feta cheese and vinaigrette, mixing well.

Amour – S'AMOURS

Here's a bonus recipe that you'll only see happen once! I saw it as elevating a rustic s'more to a fine cookie treat but KitchAnnette contributor, Joe Becwar insisted it be more of a candy confection. And two "S'mours" were born because as the movie demonstrates, it takes two! You can make one or both. They aren't "heart" at all!

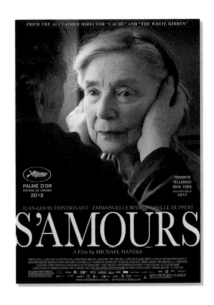

a: Version D'Une

INGREDIENTS:
- 12 oz. dark chocolate chips
- 2 1/2 cups mini marshmallows
- 1 1/2 cups graham crackers, chopped

DIRECTIONS:
1. Melt chocolate until smooth. In a large bowl, mix graham cracker bits and marshmallows. Fold in the chocolate.
2. Spread onto a wax paper-lined cookie sheet, about 1" thick. Let cool for about 10 minutes.
3. Using a heart-shaped cookie cutter, press and create hearts. Done!

b. Version À Deux

INGREDIENTS:
- 3/4 cup butter
- 3/4 cup sugar
- 1/2 cup brown sugar
- 1 tsp. cinnamon
- 1/4 cup honey
- 1 pinch salt
- 1-1/2 tsp. baking powder
- 1/2 tsp. baking soda
- 1 tsp. vanilla
- 1 large egg
- 2-1/4 cups flour
- 12 oz. dark chocolate chips
- 8 oz. mini marshmallows

DIRECTIONS:
1. Preheat oven to 375°.
2. In a large bowl, add butter, sugar, and brown sugar. Mix until well blended.
3. As it mixes, add in cinnamon, honey, salt, baking powder, baking soda, vanilla, and egg. Add flour and mix until well blended. If it's not stiff enough to roll out, let cool in the fridge 10-20 minutes.
4. Use a little flour to sprinkle where you'll roll out the dough and roll it to about 1/4" thick. Using a heart-shaped cookie cutter, press to make hearts and place on a parchment paper lined cookie sheet. Gather the remaining dough, re-roll, and cut more hearts until you've run out. Bake for about 8-9 minutes. Let cookies cool.
5. Melt marshmallows until smooth. Melt the chocolate until smooth. Create a "sandwich" by spread marshmallow onto the flat side of a cookie, then chocolate, and top with another cookie, flat side down.

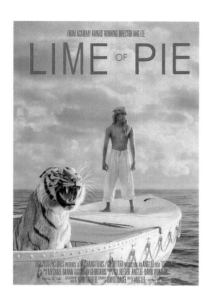

Life of Pi – LIME OF PIE

I had to do a pie. OF COURSE! We're used to hearing about key lime pie but the "key" to this pie is in using regular limes.

INGREDIENTS:
- 1/2 cup butter
- 1/3 cup sugar
- 1/4 tsp. vanilla
- 1 cup flour
- 28 oz. sweet condensed milk
- 3/4 cup lime juice
- zest of 1 lime
- 1/2 cup sour cream

DIRECTIONS:
1. Preheat oven to 450°. In a bowl, cream butter, sugar, and vanilla. Blend in flour. Spread onto bottom and sides of 9" spring form pan.
2. In a large bowl, add sweet condensed milk, lime juice, sour cream, and about 3/4 of the lime zest and mix well. Pour into the pie crust and place in oven for 8-10 minutes then lower oven to 400° and bake an additional 6-8 minutes until the center starts to show "pin bubbles". Take out and cool.
3. Remove from pan. Sprinkle the remaining lime zest over the top and serve!

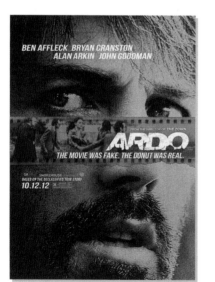

Argo – ARDO

I've found fried dough is a dessert most cultures enjoy. Using a more aromatic orange glaze distinguishes this middle-eastern version.

INGREDIENTS:
- 2 cups flour
- 4 tsp. corn starch
- 1 pinch salt
- 1/4 oz. yeast
- 1 1/4 cup water
- 1/4 tsp. sugar
- 1 cup confectioners sugar
- 2 tbsp. milk
- 1 tsp. orange juice
- zest of 1 orange
- 24 oz. canola oil

DIRECTIONS:
1. In a large bowl, mix flour, corn starch, and salt. Set aside.
2. In a separate smaller bowl, stir yeast, 1/4 cup water, and sugar. Stir this mixture into the flour mixture. Gradually add a cup of water and when it's well combined, let it sit covered for about an hour.
3. In a bowl that will be used for dipping the fried dough, mix confectioners sugar, milk, orange juice and orange zest. Set aside.
4. When the dough has risen, it's time to fry. Using a deep pot, add canola oil and turn the heat on medium-to-high.
5. When the oil is hot, carefully add a few spoonfuls of dough. Let cook until brown turning them. Keep a close eye – this may cook in a minute. Remove to a paper towel-coated dish to absorb the excess oil for a moment and coat with the orange glaze. Set aside to dry. Repeat until it's all cooked and coated. Enjoy!

My personal party night food photos:

2014

The 86th Academy Awards®   **Host: Ellen DeGeneres**
The Dolby Theater   **March 2, 2014**

This marked the 20th year since I began creating signature Oscar® menus. Quite accidentally, but very pleasingly, this meal became a decadently rich feast worthy of such a milestone. I am proud to present these recipes and look forward to the next 20 years of food and fun while celebrating film excellence!

12 Years A Slave – 12 PEARS ENCLAVED

This is an incredibly easy but amazingly rich appetizer. Feel free to change the cheese if you prefer another strong flavored variety.

INGREDIENTS:
- 2 pears
- 1/2 lb. truffle cheese
- 4 oz. baby arugula, rinsed
- 6 thin slices prosciutto

DIRECTIONS:
1. Cut pears and cheese into 12 slices. Cut each piece of proscuitto lengthwise to create 12 strips.
2. To assemble, take a piece of pear, cheese, and arugula and roll in a piece of prosciutto. Repeat for all. Plate and serve.

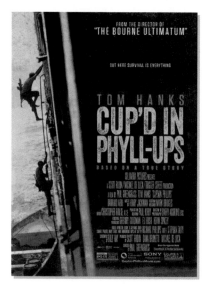

Captain Phillips – CUP'D IN PHYLL-UPS

Ok … work with me … the captain was from Maine – that's lobster waters. Did I say he was a sea captain? So we're gonna fill up the phyllo cups with lobster salad!

INGREDIENTS:
- 1 package phyllo dough, thawed
- 1 stick butter, melted
- 2 lbs. lobster meat, shredded
- 1/2 red onion, diced
- 3-4 ribs celery, chopped
- 1/2 cup mayonnaise
- salt & pepper

DIRECTIONS:
1. Preheat oven to 350°. Grease muffin tin.
2. Brush a phyllo dough sheet with butter. Add another sheet and brush it with butter. Repeat and build to 5 sheets. Cut into squares and fit into muffin tin cups. Continue until the tin is full.
3. Bake for about 10 minutes or until golden. Remove from oven and cool.
4. In a large bowl, combine lobster meat, onion, celery, mayonnaise, salt & pepper to taste.
5. Fill phyllo cups with lobster salad and serve.

Philomena – PHILETMIGNON

I love the dignity and elegance of this movie. I also love the elegance of well-prepared filet mignon with this special tarragon sauce.

INGREDIENTS:
- 3 lbs. filet mignon
- 4 tbsp. butter, divided
- salt & pepper
- 1 oz. brandy
- 1/2 tbsp. fresh tarragon
- 1/2 cup beef broth (substitute with drippings from the roasting pan)
- 3 oz. heavy cream

DIRECTIONS:
1. Preheat oven to 400°.
2. In skillet on high heat, add 2 tbsp. butter and sear all sides of the meat.
3. Transfer to a roasting pan and season the meat with salt & pepper to taste.
4. Roast for about 45 minutes or until internal temperature reaches 135°. Remove and let rest for 15 minutes.
5. In a saucepan on high heat, add 2 tbsp. butter and brandy. Burn off the alcohol and add tarragon, beef broth, heavy cream, salt & pepper to taste. Stir until well blended.
6. Slice meat into 2" thick rounds. Plate with a generous amount of sauce.

Nebraska – NEBRASKORN

There were other choices, but I had to go with a traditional corn dish but add a little bit of verve.

INGREDIENTS:
- 1 cup milk
- 1 tbsp. flour
- 1 tbsp. corn meal
- 20 oz. corn kernels
- 1 cup half & half
- 1 tsp. salt
- 1 tbsp. sugar
- 1 tsp. black pepper, freshly ground
- 4 tbsp. butter
- 1/4 cup grated Romano cheese

DIRECTIONS:
1. In a saucepan over medium heat, whisk together milk, flour, and corn meal. Add in corn, half & half, salt, sugar, pepper, butter, and cheese.
2. Keep stirring until the mixture is thickened, and corn is cooked through. Remove from heat, serve hot.

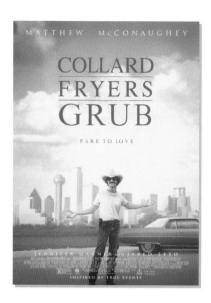

Dallas Buyers Club – COLLARD FRYERS GRUB

Collard greens are an unsung vegetable hero. They have a richness that complements so many dishes.

INGREDIENTS:
- 2 bunch collard greens
- 4 cloves garlic, chopped
- 1/2 tsp. red pepper flakes
- salt & pepper
- juice of 1 lemon
- extra virgin olive oil

DIRECTIONS:
1. Cut stems from collards. Clean to remove grit. Roll leaves and cut into strips.
2. In a large sauté pan, drizzle olive oil and on medium heat, brown garlic. Add collards, red pepper flakes, and salt & pepper to taste. Stir. Cover for 5 minutes.
3. Stir in lemon juice and cook for about 10 minutes until the greens are soft and tender. Serve warm.

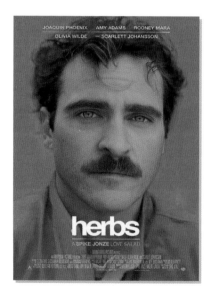

Her – HERBS

A CHICKory salad with aromatic herbs dressing ... I realize very corny (well not as corny as Nebraskorn) but it's fresh and fabulous!

INGREDIENTS:
- 1 head chicory, washed
- 1 bulb fennel, washed
- 15 oz. mandarin oranges
- 1/2 cup extra virgin olive oil
- 1/4 cup fresh lemon juice
- 1/2 tsp. chives, minced
- 1/2 tsp. basil, minced
- salt & pepper

DIRECTIONS:
1. Chop chicory and fennel. Place in a large bowl. Add oranges.
2. In a measuring cup, whisk olive oil, lemon juice, chives, basil, salt & pepper to taste.
3. Pour over salad, mix, and serve.

American Hustle – AMERICAN TRUFFLE

Ahhh... the sweet days of disco! Rich and decadent... very indulgent... very easy chocolate truffles.

INGREDIENTS:
- 1 cup heavy cream
- 8 oz. semi-sweet chocolate bits
- 8 oz. bittersweet chocolate bits
- 1 tsp. vanilla
- 1/2 cup cocoa powder

DIRECTIONS:
1. In a saucepan, heat heavy cream until it's just about to boil. Remove from heat.
2. Place chocolate in a large bowl and slowly pour in the hot cream, whisking the chocolate until melted and well blended. Add the vanilla. Place in the freezer for about 15 minutes.
3. Using a teaspoon, roll out small 1" chocolate balls, rolling quickly in your hands. Place on baking sheet and refrigerate for about 30 minutes.
4. Remove and roll in cocoa powder. Put on a dish and watch them disappear.

Gravity – BAKLAVITY

The choice of baklava for Gravity is in it's duality of being "weightless" and "heavy" in the same delectable bite. It's made with airy layers of phyllo dough and filled with a rich, dense honey and walnut delight.

INGREDIENTS:
- 3 sticks butter, divided & melted
- 3 cups walnuts, well chopped
- 2 tsp. cinnamon
- 1/4 cup sugar
- 1-1/4 cup honey
- 1 package phyllo dough, thawed

DIRECTIONS:
1. Preheat oven to 350°. In a bowl, combine walnuts, cinnamon, sugar, and honey. Melt 1-1/2 sticks butter and stir into mixture. Set aside.
2. Melt remaining butter and set aside.
3. In a clean work area, take one sheet of phyllo dough (Note: Use a damp cloth to cover unused phyllo dough sheets while assembling so they won't dry out) and brush on melted butter. Fold in half lengthwise – brush on butter. Fold again in half lengthwise & brush on butter. Spoon a "healthy" teaspoon of nut mixture on each end of the "phyllo strip". Roll in both ends towards the middle and cut in half to make two rolls. Repeat with all the sheets.
4. Place rolls on an edged baking sheet – brush tops with butter. Bake for about 20 minutes and cool on rack. Serve and enjoy!

The Wolf of Wall Street – THE POUF OF POMMES SWEET

Yeah... putting "sweet" with this movie is not the first thought. But it's more clever than it seems. Apples, the infamous "forbidden fruit" shaped into a "beggar's purse" is the irony.

INGREDIENTS:
- 3 granny smith apples, cored and peeled
- 1 red delicious apple, cored and peeled
- 1/3 cup sugar
- 1/2 tsp. cinnamon
- 1 package puffed pastry, room temperature
- 2 cups confectioners sugar
- 2 tbsp. milk

DIRECTIONS:
1. Preheat oven to 400°.
2. Cut apples into small chunks and place in a bowl. Toss with sugar and cinnamon. Set aside.
3. On a lightly floured surface, roll out pastry sheets to 12" x 12" and cut into four squares.
4. Spoon a heaping tablespoon of apples into the center of one square. Gather the ends towards to top and twist closed. Add a couple of small slits and place in a greased muffin tin. Repeat until you've used all the dough and apples.
5. Bake for 12-15 minutes or until they are golden brown. Let cool in pan for 5 minutes before placing on cooling rack.
6. Mix confectioners sugar and milk in a small bowl to make icing. Drizzle the "neck" of the pouf with icing and let dry. Serve and enjoy.

My personal party night food photos:

MEAL INDEX

APPETIZERS:

MAIN COURSES:

MEAL INDEX

SIDE DISHES:

SALADS:

MEAL INDEX

DESSERTS:

ABOUT THE AUTHOR

A native New Yorker, Annette was born into the food business, even rolling meatballs for her dad's catering jobs by the age of 5! From her family's beloved Bronx neighborhood deli, Nancy's Delicatessen, and Manhattan restaurants, to the wholesale produce industry, she knows food. Although she pursued and enjoyed a career in marketing/advertising, she never lost her zest for cooking, entertaining, and all things food. She switched gears to join the family produce business before creating KitchAnnette™. Her passion is to show how engaging and easy the kitchen can be.

Annette launched JUICE THIS™ Perfectly Portioned Produce Packs in July 2013. She also writes the blog, KitchAnnette™ "Dishin' the Dish" and is developing new kitchen products.

She lives in New York.